Philokalia

The Eastern Christian

Spiritual Texts

Books in the SkyLight Illuminations Series

The Art of War—Spirituality for Conflict: Annotated & Explained
Bhagavad Gita: Annotated & Explained
The Book of Mormon: Selections Annotated & Explained
Dhammapada: Annotated & Explained
The Divine Feminine in Biblical Wisdom Literature:
    Selections Annotated & Explained
Ecclesiastes: Annotated & Explained
The End of Days: Essential Selections from
    Apocalyptic Texts—Annotated & Explained
Ethics of the Sages: Pirke Avot—Annotated & Explained
Ghazali on the Principles of Islamic Spirituality: Selections from
    Forty Foundations of Religion—Annotated & Explained
Gnostic Writings on the Soul: Annotated & Explained
The Gospel of Philip: Annotated & Explained
The Gospel of Thomas: Annotated & Explained
Hasidic Tales: Annotated & Explained
The Hebrew Prophets: Selections Annotated & Explained
The Hidden Gospel of Matthew: Annotated & Explained
The Infancy Gospels of Jesus: Apocryphal Tales from
    the Childhoods of Mary and Jesus—Annotated & Explained
The Lost Sayings of Jesus: Teachings from Ancient Christian, Jewish,
    Gnostic and Islamic Sources—Annotated & Explained
The Meditations of Marcus Aurelius: Selections Annotated & Explained
Native American Stories of the Sacred: Annotated & Explained
Philokalia: The Eastern Christian Spiritual Texts—Annotated & Explained
The Qur'an and Sayings of Prophet Muhammad:
    Selections Annotated & Explained
Rumi and Islam: Selections from His Stories, Poems,
    and Discourses—Annotated & Explained
The Sacred Writings of Paul: Selections Annotated & Explained
Saint Augustine of Hippo: Selections from Confessions and
    Other Essential Writings—Annotated & Explained
The Secret Book of John: The Gnostic Gospel—Annotated & Explained
Selections from the Gospel of Sri Ramakrishna: Annotated & Explained
Sex Texts from the Bible: Selections Annotated & Explained
Spiritual Writings on Mary: Annotated & Explained
Tao Te Ching: Annotated & Explained
Tanya, the Masterpiece of Hasidic Wisdom: Selections Annotated & Explained
The Way of a Pilgrim: The Jesus Prayer Journey—Annotated & Explained
Zohar: Annotated & Explained

Philokalia

The Eastern Christian Spiritual Texts

Selections Annotated & Explained

Annotation by Allyne Smith

Translation by G. E. H. Palmer, Philip Sherrard,
and Bishop Kallistos Ware

Walking Together, Finding the Way®
SKYLIGHT PATHS®
PUBLISHING

Philokalia: The Eastern Christian Spiritual Texts—Selections Annotated & Explained

2010 Quality Paperback Edition

For information regarding permission to reprint material from this book, please mail or fax your request in writing to SkyLight Paths Publishing, Permissions Department, at the address / fax number listed below, or e-mail your request to permissions@skylightpaths.com.

Grateful acknowledgment is given for permission to use material from the following sources:

THE PHILOKALIA: THE COMPLETE TEXT VOLUMES I–IV compiled by St. Nikodimos of the Holy Mountain and St. Makarios of Corinth, translated by G.E.H. Palmer, Philip Sherrard, and Kallistos Ware. Translation copyright (c) 1979, 1981, 1984, 1995 by the Eling Trust. Reprinted by permission of Faber and Faber, Inc., an affiliate of Farrar, Straus and Giroux, LLC.

Annotation and introductory material © 2006 by Allyne Smith

Library of Congress Cataloging-in-Publication Data

Smith, Allyne.

Philokalia : the Eastern Christian spiritual texts : annotated & explained / annotation by Allyne Smith ; translation by G. E. H. Palmer, Philip Sherrard, and Kallistos Ware.

p. cm. — (SkyLight illuminations series)

Includes bibliographical references.

ISBN-13: 978-1-59473-103-7 (quality pbk.)

ISBN-10: 1-59473-103-9 (quality pbk.)

1. Philokalia. 2. Spiritual life—Orthodox Eastern Church—Early works to 1800.
3. Orthodox Eastern Church—Doctrines. I. Title. II. Series: SkyLight illuminations.

BX382.S58 2006

248.4'819—dc22

2006017643

Manufactured in the United States of America

Cover Design: Walter C. Bumford III. Cover Art: © Matjaz Slanic, courtesy of www.istockphoto.com.

SkyLight Paths Publishing is creating a place where people of different spiritual traditions come together for challenge and inspiration, a place where we can help each other understand the mystery that lies at the heart of our existence.

SkyLight Paths sees both believers and seekers as a community that increasingly transcends traditional boundaries of religion and denomination—people wanting to learn from each other, *walking together, finding the way.*

SkyLight Paths, "Walking Together, Finding the Way" and colophon are trademarks of LongHill Partners, Inc., registered in the U.S. Patent and Trademark Office.

Walking Together, Finding the Way®

Published by SkyLight Paths Publishing

An Imprint of Turner Publishing Company

4507 Charlotte Avenue, Suite 100

Nashville, TN 37209

Tel: (615) 255-2665

www.skylightpaths.com

Contents □

For my parents,
who first taught me to love the beautiful

Introduction ☐

Virtually every spiritual tradition has an authoritative scripture or scriptures that serve as a foundational text for its beliefs, practices, and spirituality. For Christians, that collection of texts is the Holy Bible. But the fracturing of the Christian Church in the fifth century (following the Council of Chalcedon in 451), the eleventh century (the break between what came to be known as the Eastern Orthodox and Roman Catholic Churches), and the sixteenth century (the Protestant Reformation) has produced a dizzying variety of spiritual traditions. Each of these traditions in turn has its own set of subsidiary texts that serve as spiritual classics within the particular tradition. These secondary texts give expression to each tradition's appropriation of the Bible. Each spiritual tradition reflects a lived interpretation of scripture.

For the Eastern Orthodox Churches, the principal spiritual text has come to be the *Philokalia,* an anthology of older texts edited by Nikodimos of the Holy Mountain (1749–1809) and Makarios of Corinth (1731–1805) and published in 1782. These monks of the Greek Orthodox Church collected sayings on prayer and spirituality from Eastern, mostly monastic writers that span more than a millennium, from the fourth to the fifteenth centuries. The *Philokalia,* more than any other text, reflects the Eastern Church's interpretation of the Bible's meaning. In the anonymous nineteenth-century Russian classic *The Way of a Pilgrim,* the pilgrim asks a *staretz,* or spiritual father, whether the *Philokalia* is "more exalted and holier than the Bible." The *staretz* answers:

> No, it is not more exalted or holier than the Bible, but it contains enlightened explanations of what is mystically contained in the Bible, and it is so lofty that it is not easily comprehended by our shortsighted

intellects. Let me give you an illustration. The sun is the greatest, the most resplendent and magnificent source of light, but you cannot contemplate or examine it with the simple naked eye. You would need to use a special viewing lens, which, though a million times smaller and dimmer than the sun, would enable you to study this magnificent source of all light and to endure and delight in its fiery rays. Thus the Holy Scriptures are like a brilliant sun, for which the *Philokalia* is the lens needed in order to view it.[1]

Philokalia is a Greek word meaning "love of the beautiful." Two of the Cappadocian Fathers, Gregory the Theologian (329–389) and Basil the Great (c. 330–379), edited a collection of the writings of Origen, the great third-century theologian of Alexandria, and gave it the title *Philokalia*. In subsequent centuries, other small works of monastic spirituality also took the same title. The full name of the present text is *The Philokalia of the Neptic Saints gathered from our Holy Theophoric* ["God-bearing"] *Fathers, through which, by means of the philosophy of ascetic practice and contemplation, the intellect is purified, illumined, and made perfect*—a title that serves not only to distinguish it from the earlier collections but also calls attention to the importance of "watchfulness" (translating the Greek *nepsis*) for the spiritual tradition represented in the work of Nikodimos and Makarios.

The Monks of Mount Athos

Nikodimos and Makarios were both monks of Mount Athos, an autonomous monastic republic located on a peninsula in northeastern Greece. It is generally regarded as the most important center of Orthodox monasticism. Although the first formal monasteries were founded in the tenth century, Athos had already attracted monks such as Peter the Athonite and Euthymios the Younger in the ninth century.

The contemplative tradition of the Holy Mountain (as Mount Athos is known in Greece) had reached its height in the fourteenth century, but by the seventeenth it had become prey to secularizing influences from the West. Realizing the danger to the authentic spiritual character of Mount

Athos, the leaders of the Athonite monasteries sought to recover its true heritage. One leader in this was Nikodimos. Although best remembered for the *Philokalia,* he authored or translated over a hundred books on the spiritual life. Makarios, a fellow monk who later left the Holy Mountain to become archbishop of Corinth, aided him in the compilation of the *Philokalia.*

The Eastern Christian spiritual tradition is not composed of "schools" as in the West, where they are typically associated with a particular religious order (for example, Benedictine, Carmelite, or Franciscan). Yet there is more than one approach in the East. The one favored on Athos is known as hesychasm, from the Greek word *hesychia,* translated as "stillness." It flourished especially in the fourteenth century on Athos, at a time when a controversy arose over the experience of God. An Italian monk named Barlaam was teaching in Constantinople and in Greece and, after visiting the monks on Mount Athos, he began challenging both the legitimacy of mental prayer and the Athonite belief that the monks experienced the uncreated light of Mount Tabor, that is, the light of the Transfiguration of Christ. Barlaam argued instead that the light was material and created. For the Athonites, this was tantamount to denying that the monks experienced God himself. Gregory Palamas (1296–1359), a monk of Athos and later archbishop of Thessaloniki, became the spokesman for the Holy Mountain. In his defense of their position, he reiterated the Eastern Christian distinction between the essence and energies of God. We cannot experience the essence of God, but we can experience God's energies, that is, God's actions in the world. These energies—including the Taboric light—are divine and uncreated. Thus we can experience God in God's energies, and not simply something created outside of God.

Mount Athos continues to be the home of twenty monasteries and at least a dozen *sketes* (smaller communities of monks). Only monks may live on Athos, and female visitors are not permitted. About two thousand monks live on Athos today. While the great number of visitors to the Holy Mountain can become a distraction for the monks, they nonetheless seek to maintain the silent character of their life. John Chryssavgis in his recent book *Light through Darkness: The Orthodox Tradition* describes their typical daily schedule:

> A bell rings in the silence of the night at about midnight, calling monks to silent prayer and study. A wooden gong sounds at 4 a.m., inviting monks to worship (Matins and Liturgy, normally on a daily basis) in the silence of the night. The monks proceed silently to the refectory, where lunch follows in silence at 8:00 a.m. There is a brief period of rest and quiet. From 10:00 a.m. to 4:00 p.m., the monks work in silence. Vespers is at 5:00 p.m. The evening meal, again in silence, is at 6:00 p.m. There may follow a spell of relaxation from work and silence, when monks mingle with one another or with visitors on the balconies. Compline in the main church is held at 7:00 p.m. Afterwards the monks retire in complete silence to their cells.[2]

Theology in the Eastern Tradition

Western Christians often compartmentalize the spiritual from the theological. In the East, however, there is a holistic view of theology. Dogmatic or systematic theology (which deals with beliefs about God), liturgical theology (worship), moral theology (ethics), and spiritual/ascetical theology are all aspects of a singular enterprise. Moreover, dogmatic theology is meant to be lived. Vladimir Lossky (1903–1958) gave classic expression to this traditional understanding.

> We must live the dogma expressing a revealed truth, which appears to us as an unfathomable mystery, in such a fashion that instead of assimilating the mystery to our mode of understanding, we should, on the contrary, look for a profound change, an inner transformation of spirit, enabling us to experience it mystically. Far from being mutually opposed, theology and mysticism support and complete each other. If the mystical experience is a personal working out of the content of the common faith, theology is an expression, for the profit of all, of that which can be experienced by everyone. Outside the truth kept by the whole Church personal experience would be deprived of all certainty, of all objectivity. It would be a mingling of truth and

falsehood, of reality and of illusion: "mysticism" in the bad sense of the word. On the other hand, the teaching of the Church would have no hold on souls if it did not in some degree express an inner experience of truth, granted in different measure to each one of the faithful. There is, therefore, no Christian mysticism without theology; but, above all, there is no theology without mysticism.[3]

This is simply an elaboration of the saying of Evagrios contained in the *Philokalia*: "If you are a theologian, you will pray truly. And if you pray truly, you are a theologian."

The spiritual teaching of the Fathers of the Holy Mountain is grounded in the Eastern Church's theological anthropology. The human being is a fundamental unity of body and soul and should be understood as an "embodied soul" or an "ensouled body." The Eastern spiritual tradition takes our psychosomatic nature quite seriously, so that worship and prayer draw on our body and all its senses. Even the inward act of repentance is expressed outwardly with bows, prostrations, and signs of the cross.

The soul is understood as having more than one faculty. For our purposes, the important distinction to draw is between the faculty of *dianoia* and that of the *nous*. The *dianoia* is understood as being responsible for discursive reasoning, the faculty we use, for instance, in logic and mathematics. But the *nous* is the spiritual aspect of the psyche, the faculty through which we experience God. Latin theologians such as Thomas Aquinas preserved this distinction, translating *dianoia* as *ratio* ("reason") and *nous* as *intellectus* ("intellect"). But since *reason* and *intellect* are used almost synonymously these days, it is important to understand how the two terms are used in the *Philokalia* and other Eastern Christian texts.

The *nous* is "the eye of the soul," the very heart of what it means to be a person made in the image and likeness of God. It is the spiritual faculty through which we directly experience God. Darkened by the fall, the *nous* must be purified through watchfulness, prayer, and other spiritual practices.

It is also important to understand that the Eastern view of humanity is more positive than the traditional Western view. Augustine's view of original sin, which has been so influential in the West, is largely unknown to Orthodox theology, which prefers to speak of "ancestral sin." There is no inherited guilt. And, unlike Calvinism, the Eastern tradition does not see the human person as "totally depraved." While human sin may obscure the image of God within us, it can never erase that image; and while pursuing a life free from sin may inhibit our choices, sin cannot eradicate our fundamental human freedom. While the Orthodox tradition believes that God is utterly transcendent, it "no less insists on His total and ineradicable presence in man and in every other form of created existence."[4]

The *Philokalia's* Approach to Salvation

In this edition, I have identified seven themes that recur throughout the *Philokalia*—repentance, the heart, prayer, the Jesus Prayer, the passions, stillness, and *theosis,* or deification. The last of these themes requires more explanation than the rest.

Theosis, usually rendered in English as "deification" or "divinization," is at the core of how Eastern Christians understand salvation. Much of the Christian West seems to understand salvation as salvation *from* something (hell). In one common view associated with Anselm of Canterbury, who applied medieval social thinking to soteriology (the theology of salvation), the severity of a sin is measured not by the intrinsic quality of the sin, but by the status of the person against whom the sin is committed.

Thus, a minor theft against a fellow peasant might not be considered very serious, but the same theft, if it involved a possession of the king, could warrant the death penalty. Applied to soteriology, human sin has caused an infinite violation against God's justice, because God is infinite. Human beings, who are finite, cannot possibly pay the infinite penalty demanded for our transgression. Therefore, God provides his Son, Jesus (who is also infinite), to pay the penalty for human sin on the cross. The righteousness of Christ is then imputed to humans who, even though

nothing has changed for them on this account (they are still miserable sinners), will now be seen by God *as if* they were Christ. This act of justification is seen as the essential soteriological transaction, although some
(such as John and Charles Wesley) will see the process of sanctification
as equally essential.

The East, along with many in the West, understands salvation as a
sharing in God's life, a participation in the Divine. One way of saying this
would be to say that the East holds both justification (restoration of a right
relationship with God) and sanctification (growth in holiness) as two sides
of the coin of salvation. But more must be said about how the East understands sanctification, for it has never shied away from the bold language
of deification. The Eastern writers, of course, look to the language of the
New Testament, particularly 2 Peter 1:4, wherein Peter declares that we
are to become "partakers of the divine nature."

At the same time, they look to the early witness of the Church at a
time before the New Testament canon was finally set. Irenaeus of Lyons,
originally from Asia Minor but known for his days as a bishop in France
and his theological writings as bishop, is an important witness. He learned
the Christian faith from Polycarp, who in turn had known John, the apostle of Jesus. In his presentation of the apostolic faith, *Against the Heresies,*
Irenaeus says unequivocally that "For it was for this end that the Word
of God was made man, and He who was the Son of God became the
Son of man, that man, having been taken into the Word, and receiving
the adoption, might become the son of God." Athanasios of Alexandria,
who was the first person to list the canon of the New Testament as we
now have it (in the year 367!), echoed this when he wrote in *On the
Incarnation* that "he, indeed, assumed humanity that we might become
God." Basil of Caesarea, also in the fourth century, tells us that the human
being is the only creature to have received the order to become a god.

This is the soteriology inherited by the writers of the *Philokalia.* When
this teaching was attacked in the fourteenth century, Gregory Palamas of
Mount Athos was called upon to defend its truth. He emphasized the

distinction between God's essence (which is inaccessible) and God's ener-gies—God's actions in creation and in human beings (which are truly God but which we can experience). Thus, through the process of *theosis*, we become by grace what God is by nature.

The *Philokalia*'s Influence
Outside Greece, the *Philokalia*'s influence spread, especially to Russia and Romania. Paisii Velichovsky (1722–1794) spent sixteen years on Mount Athos and then became an abbot of a monastery in Moldavia. During his years as an abbot, he translated a selection of *Philokalia* texts into Slavonic. It was this one-volume edition, printed with the Slavonic title *Dobrotolubie*, that was carried by the anonymous author of *The Way of a Pilgrim*. Complete translations of the *Philokalia* into Russian were made by Ignatius Brianchaninov (1807–1867) and Theophan the Recluse (1815–1894). The spiritual approach of the *Philokalia* was popularized by *The Way of a Pilgrim*.

The priest and theologian Dumitru Staniloae (1903–1993) translated the *Philokalia* into Romanian, where it became an important influence in the revival of both monastic and lay spirituality. In our own day, the hesychastic spirituality of the *Philokalia* has played a significant role in the revival of contemplative prayer and the form of contemplation known as Centering Prayer, influencing the Trappist monk and author Thomas Merton (1915–1968). The increasing practice of contemplative prayer was further encouraged from the 1970s on by Thomas Keating and M. Basil Pennington, as a Christian alternative to Zen Buddhist meditation, thus bringing Western Christians back to the Jesus Prayer of the Eastern tradition.

About the Translation
The translation used in this edition is that prepared by the late G. E. H. Palmer, the late Philip Sherrard, and Bishop Kallistos Ware, and published by Faber and Faber. It is used with the kind permission of Bishop Kallistos and the publisher.

Philokalia

The Eastern Christian

Spiritual Texts

1 Here Isaiah the Solitary expresses the same confidence that Paul speaks of in Romans 8:38–39, that "nothing can separate us from the love of God." All that is required is for the sinner to repent and return to God.

2 Notice that the grammar here suggests it is not the person but the person's sins that deserve eternal punishment. The texts of the liturgy remind the faithful repeatedly that even though our sins merit punishment, God is love and it is God's nature to be merciful.

3 Here Mark the Ascetic is citing 1 John 5:16. While the Roman Catholic tradition has identified particular acts as "mortal" sins, in the Orthodox tradition we see that only a sin for which we don't repent is "mortal."

4 Mark suggests that salvation, while the work of God, nonetheless requires our participation. In the Orthodox tradition this is called *synergism,* a term that derives from the biblical statement of St. Peter that we are "cooperators" with God (*synergoi*).

1 □ Repentance

Be attentive to yourself, so that nothing destructive can separate you from the love of God. Guard your heart, and do not grow listless and say: "How shall I guard it, since I am a sinner?" For when a man abandons his sins and returns to God, his repentance regenerates him and renews him entirely.[1]

St. Isaiah the Solitary
I, On Guarding the Intellect, Sec. 22

Until a man is completely changed by repentance, he will be wise always to remember his sins with sorrow and to recall the eternal fire that they justly deserve.[2]

Evagrios the Solitary
I, On Prayer, Sec. 144

There is a sin that is always "unto death": the sin for which we do not repent. For this sin even a saint's prayers will not be heard.[3]

St. Mark the Ascetic
I, On Those Who Think that They Are Made
Righteous by Works, Sec. 41

He who repents rightly does not imagine that it is his own effort that cancels his former sins; but through this effort he makes his peace with God.[4]

St. Mark the Ascetic
I, On Those Who Think that They Are Made
Righteous by Works, Sec. 42

5 While the prayers of the Orthodox Christian do not exhibit a morbid preoccupation with sin, they *are* characterized by repentance. This is not to be understood primarily as emotional regret for sin but rather as the person's "change of mind."

6 Neilos the Ascetic (died ca. 430) was probably from Constantinople and a follower of St. John Chrysostom. He became abbot of a monastery in what is now Ankara, Turkey, and is the first writer known to make unequivocal mention of the Jesus Prayer.

Each hour of the day we should note and weigh our actions and in the evening we should do what we can to free ourselves of the burden of them by means of repentance—if, that is, we wish, with God's help, to overcome wickedness. We should also make sure that we perform all our outward tasks in a manner that accords with God's will, before God and for God alone, so that we are not mindlessly seduced by the senses.[5]

ST. HESYCHIOS THE PRIEST
I, ON *WATCHFULNESS AND HOLINESS*, SEC. 124

In the biblical story Elisha then threw a stick into the Jordan and brought to the surface the axe-head his disciple had lost (cf. 2 Kings 6:6); that is to say, he revealed a thought that his disciple believed to be hidden deep within him and he exposed it to the view of those present. Here the Jordan signifies speaking about repentance, for it was in the Jordan that John performed the baptism of repentance. Now if someone does not speak accurately about repentance, but makes his listeners despise it by failing to communicate its hidden power, he lets the axe-head fall into the Jordan. But then a stick—and this signifies the cross—brings the axe-head up from the depths to the surface. For prior to the cross the full meaning of repentance was hidden, and anyone who tried to say something about it could easily be convicted of speaking rashly and inadequately. After the Crucifixion, however, the meaning of repentance became clear to all, for it had been revealed at the appointed time through the wood of the cross.

ST. NEILOS THE ASCETIC[6]
I, *ASCETIC DISCOURSE*

7 Here John stresses an important aspect of Orthodox anthropology: despite our sins, we never lose the image of God in which we are created. Unlike some Western theology, which sees the human being as "totally depraved," the East believes that repentance will return a person to his or her "true splendor"—the image of God.

LXX is an abbreviation for the Septuagint, the Greek edition of the Hebrew Bible that has always been the authoritative Old Testament of the Orthodox Church.

8 Here Maximos suggests that the people sin "in relation to intelligence." By *intelligence* he is referring to the *nous* ("intellect")—the aspect of the human psyche that is the faculty for communion with God.

The moon as it waxes and wanes illustrates the condition of man: sometimes he does what is right, sometimes he sins and then through repentance returns to a holy life. The intellect of one who sins is not destroyed (as some of you think), just as the physical size of the moon does not diminish, but only its light. Through repentance a man regains his true splendor, just as the moon after the period of waning clothes itself once more in its full light. If a man believes in Christ, "Even though he dies, he shall live" (John 11:25); he shall know that "I the Lord have spoken, and will do it" (Ezekiel 17:24, LXX).[7]

ST. JOHN OF KARPATHOS
I, *FOR THE ENCOURAGEMENT OF THE MONKS IN
INDIA WHO HAD WRITTEN TO HIM*, SEC. 4

Observe, with reference to this passage from Jonah (3:1–9), how the king represents the natural law. The throne is an impassioned disposition in alliance with the senses. The robe is the display of self-esteem. Sackcloth is the grief of repentance. Ashes are humility. Men are those who sin in relation to intelligence; beasts those who sin in relation to desire; cattle those who sin in relation to their incensive power; and sheep those who sin in relation to the contemplation of visible things.[8]

ST. MAXIMOS THE CONFESSOR
II, *FOURTH CENTURY OF VARIOUS TEXTS*, SEC. 95

9 Theognostos emphasizes two important truths that are often obscured. First, God is "angry" at our sins but not at us. Second, he immediately goes on to point out the metaphorical nature of such language about God. God "is beyond passion and vengefulness."

10 Theognostos (fourteenth century?) is known to us only as the author of the work included in the *Philokalia*.

We will not be punished or condemned in the age to be because we have sinned, since we were given a mutable and unstable nature. But we will be punished if, after sinning, we did not repent and turn from our evil ways to the Lord; for we have been given the power to repent, as well as the time in which to do so. Only through repentance shall we receive God's mercy, and not its opposite, his passionate anger. Not that God is angry with us: he is angry with evil. Indeed, the Divine is beyond passion and vengefulness, though we speak of it as reflecting, like a mirror, our actions and dispositions, giving to each of us whatever we deserve.[9]

St. Theognostos[10]

II, *On the Practice of the Virtues*, sec. 47

When you fall from a higher state, do not become panic-stricken, but through remorse, grief, rigorous self-reproach, and, above all, through copious tears shed in a contrite spirit, correct yourself and return quickly to your former condition. Rising up again after your fall, you will enter the joyous valley of salvation, taking care so far as possible not to anger your Judge again, so as not to need atoning tears and sorrow in the future. But if you show no such repentance in this present life, you will certainly be punished in the age to be.

St. Theognostos

II, *On the Practice of the Virtues*, sec. 48

Those who deliberately refuse to repent sin continually; those who sin without meaning to not only repent with all their heart, but also do not often have cause to repent.

Ilias the Presbyter

III, *A Gnomic Anthology*, sec. 14

11 One of the gifts of baptism is the forgiveness of sins. Repentance is a "second baptism" that restores the grace of baptism.

12 Peter exhorts sinners not to despair and challenges their belief that the Creator of all is incapable of saving them. Because God is, as the liturgy says, "the lover of mankind," because Paul tells us that it is God's desire "that all shall be saved" (1 Timothy 2:3–4), so we should not lose hope.

13 Although we usually find the Eastern writers stressing that the key to salvation is repentance, it is often mentioned along with humility. In this passage, Peter suggests that even if people cannot manage to repent, they can nonetheless be saved by humility. Before receiving Holy Communion, Orthodox Christians profess their belief that "Christ came into the world to save sinners, of whom I am the first." This will lead to the person not daring "to judge or censure anyone."

If from the start we had wanted to keep the commandments and to remain as we were when baptized, we would not have fallen into so many sins or have needed the trials and tribulations of repentance. If we so wish, however, God's second gift of grace—repentance—can lead us back to our former beauty.[11] But if we fail to repent, inevitably we will depart with the unrepentant demons into agelong punishment, more by our own free choice than against our will. Yet God did not create us for wrath but for salvation (cf. 1 Thessalonians 5:9), so that we might enjoy his blessings; and we should therefore be thankful and grateful toward our Benefactor. But our failure to get to know his gifts has made us indolent, and indolence has made us forgetful, with the result that ignorance lords it over us. We have to make strenuous efforts when we first try to return to where we fell from.

St. Peter of Damaskos
III, *A Treasury of Divine Knowledge*, Introduction

Even if you are not what you should be, you should not despair. It is bad enough that you have sinned; why in addition do you wrong God by regarding him in your ignorance as powerless? Is he, who for your sake created the great universe that you behold, incapable of saving your soul?[12] And if you say that this fact, as well as his incarnation, only makes your condemnation worse, then repent; and he will receive your repentance, as he accepted that of the prodigal son (Luke 15:20) and the prostitute (Luke 7:37–50). But if repentance is too much for you, and you sin out of habit even when you do not want to, show humility like the publican (Luke 18:13): this is enough to ensure your salvation.[13] For he who sins without repenting, yet does not despair, must of necessity regard himself as the lowest of creatures, and will not dare to judge or censure anyone. Rather, he will marvel at God's compassion.

St. Peter of Damaskos
III, *A Treasury of Divine Knowledge*,
That We Should Not Despair Even if We Sin Many Times

14 God is better understood as a physician than as a judge, just as sin is better understood as illness than as transgression. In the mystery of repentance (sacramental confession), this is the image used. The penitent come before God and the priest (as God's agent) not to plead guilty but to seek healing. Indeed, the priest exhorts the penitent to leave nothing unconfessed, "lest having come to a Physician" they leave unhealed.

It is always possible to make a new start by means of repentance. "You fell," it is written, "now arise" (Proverbs 24:16). And if you fall again, then rise again, without despairing at all of your salvation, no matter what happens. As long as you do not surrender yourself willingly to the enemy, your patient endurance, combined with self-reproach, will suffice for your salvation. "For at one time we ourselves went astray in our folly and disobedience," says St. Paul. "... Yet he saved us, not because of any good things we had done, but in his mercy" (Titus 3:5). So do not despair in any way, ignoring God's help, for he can do whatever he wishes. On the contrary, place your hope in him and he will do one of these things: either through trials and temptations, or in some other way which he alone knows, he will bring about your restoration; or he will accept your patient endurance and humility in the place of works; or because of your hope he will act lovingly toward you in some other way of which you are not aware, and so will save your shackled soul. Only do not abandon your Physician.**14**

ST. PETER OF DAMASKOS
III, *THE GREAT BENEFIT OF TRUE REPENTANCE*

For these good things we ought all of us always to give thanks to him, especially those who have received from him the power to renew their holy baptism through repentance, because without repentance no one can be saved. For the Lord has said, "Why do you call me, Lord, Lord, yet fail to do the things I tell you?" (Luke 6:46).

ST. PETER OF DAMASKOS
III, *HOW IT IS IMPOSSIBLE TO BE SAVED WITHOUT HUMILITY*

15 Anger separates us from God; Peter goes as far as to say that arguing puts us out of the Church and out of communion with God.

16 It is common for Orthodox Christians, especially monastics, to perform prostrations as an outward sign of their repentance. Peter reiterates the unchanging teaching of the Church that such outward signs are worthless unless they embody true repentance.

17 John Chrysostom (ca. 347–407) was archbishop of Constantinople. He is counted among the Three Holy Hierarchs (along with St. Basil the Great and St. Gregory the Theologian).

In this way everyone may know that when he argues he is outside of all the churches and estranged from God.**15** He has need of that one marvelous act of repentance, and if he fails to make that genuinely, and so remains unrepentant, not even a thousand prostrations will help him.**16** For repentance, properly speaking, is the eradication of evil, says St. John Chrysostom;**17** while what are called acts of repentance or prostrations are a bending of the knees, which expresses the fact that the person who bows sincerely before God and man after having offended someone assumes the attitude of a servant. By doing this he can claim in self-defense that he has not answered back at all or attempted to justify himself, as did the Pharisee, but is more like the publican in considering himself the least of all men and unworthy to lift his eyes to heaven (Luke 18:11–13). For if he thinks he is repentant and nevertheless attempts to refute the person who—rightly or wrongly—is judging him, he is not worthy of the grace of forgiveness, since he acts as if he seeks a hearing in court and the opportunity to justify himself, hoping to achieve what he wants through due process of law. Such behavior is entirely at odds with the Lord's commandments.... In such a case grace is no longer our guiding principle—the grace that justifies the ungodly without the works of righteousness (Romans 4:5), but only on condition that we are grateful for rebukes and endure them with forbearance, giving thanks to those who rebuke us and remaining patient and unresentful before our accusers. In this way our prayer will be pure and our repentance effective. For the more we pray for those who slander and accuse us, the more God pacifies those who bear enmity toward us and also gives us peace through our pure and persistent prayer.

St. Peter of Damaskos
III, *A Treasury of Divine Knowledge*, Spurious Knowledge

18 Makarios emphasizes that because God is love, God always "awaits with great patience the repentance of every sinner.... " At the same time, he warns of the danger of taking God's forgiveness for granted, not because God will change his mind about forgiving, but because we might grow so distant from God that we might no longer feel the need to repent.

19 Symeon the New Theologian (949–1022) was a mystic and ascetic who also served as abbot of St. Mamas Monastery from ca. 980 to 1005. His work stressed the direct experience of the Holy Spirit. The experience of the Spirit as light is emphasized in his many works, which were influential in Orthodox monasteries of the fourteenth and fifteenth centuries.

Being bountiful and full of love, God awaits with great patience the repentance of every sinner, and he celebrates the return of the sinner with celestial rejoicing; as he himself says, "There is joy in heaven over one sinner who repents" (Luke 15:7, 10). But when someone sees this generosity and patience, and how God awaits repentance and so does not punish sins one by one, he may neglect the commandment and make such generosity an excuse for indifference, adding sin to sin, offense to offense, laziness to laziness. In this way he will reach the furthest limits of sin, and fall into such transgression that he is not able to recover himself.[18]

ST. MAKARIOS OF EGYPT
III, *THE RAISING OF THE INTELLECT*, SEC. 71

"Let no one deceive you with vain words" (Ephesians 5:6), and let us not deceive ourselves: before we have experienced inward grief and tears there is no true repentance or change of mind in us, nor is there any fear of God in our hearts, nor have we passed sentence on ourselves, nor has our soul become conscious of the coming judgment and eternal torments. Had we accused ourselves and realized these things in ourselves, we would have immediately shed tears; for without tears our hardened hearts cannot be mollified, our souls cannot acquire spiritual humility, and we cannot be humble. If we do not attain such a state, we cannot be united with the Holy Spirit. And if we have not been united with the Holy Spirit through purification, we cannot have either vision or knowledge of God, or be initiated into the hidden virtues of humility.

ST. SYMEON THE NEW THEOLOGIAN[19]
IV, *PRACTICAL AND THEOLOGICAL TEXTS*, SEC. 69

20 Baptism is not magic. It requires our cooperation with God's grace. It is thus possible to lose our sanctification and our salvation (Hebrews 6:4–5).

21 A hallmark of the Orthodox tradition in general and of the monastic tradition represented in the *Philokalia* in particular is the emphasis on the spiritual father or mother. Symeon believed that a true spiritual father is one who has the *charism* ("gift") of hearing confessions and pronouncing absolution. The Church, however, associates the ministry of absolution with the ordained ministries of bishop and priest.

22 Repentance is never finished; it is something that is to be practiced daily.

23 The Gospel of Matthew contains the exhortation of Jesus that we must first be reconciled before approaching the altar (Matthew 5:23–24).

Through holy baptism we are granted remission of our sins, are freed from the ancient curse, and are sanctified by the presence of the Holy Spirit. But we do not as yet receive the perfection of grace … for that is true only of those who are steadfast in faith and have demonstrated this through what they do. If after we have been baptized we gravitate toward evil and foul actions, we lose the sanctification of baptism completely. But through repentance, confession, and tears we receive a corresponding remission of our former sins and, in this way, sanctification accompanied by the grace of God.[20]

ST. SYMEON THE NEW THEOLOGIAN
IV, *PRACTICAL AND THEOLOGICAL TEXTS*, SEC. 74

Through repentance the filth of our foul actions is washed away. After this, we participate in the Holy Spirit, not automatically, but according to the faith, humility, and inner disposition of the repentance in which our soul is engaged. In addition, we must also have received complete remission of our sins from our spiritual father.[21] For this reason it is good to repent each day, in accordance with the commandment that tells us to do this; for the words, "Repent, for the kingdom of heaven has drawn near" (Matthew 3:2), indicate that the act of repentance is unending.[22]

ST. SYMEON THE NEW THEOLOGIAN
IV, *PRACTICAL AND THEOLOGICAL TEXTS*, SEC. 75

Take care never to receive communion while you have anything against anyone, even if this is only a hostile thought.[23] Not until you have brought about reconciliation through repentance should you communicate. But you will learn this, too, through prayer.

ST. SYMEON THE NEW THEOLOGIAN
IV, *PRACTICAL AND THEOLOGICAL TEXTS*, SEC. 132

24 Nikitas Stithatos (eleventh century) was the biographer of Symeon. Nikitas entered the Studios monastery of Constantinople. At the request of Symeon, he made copies of the latter's writings, which he later edited and circulated. Because of his frank criticism of the emperor Constantine IX Monomachos's illicit sexual affair, he was nicknamed "courageous" (*Stithatos*). He wrote a number of theological and spiritual treatises, which showed the strong influence of Symeon. He may have served as abbot of Studios in the years before his death.

Sometimes the flow of tears produces an acrid and painful feeling in the heart's organ of spiritual perception; sometimes it induces delight and a sense of jubilation. Thus, when through repentance we are in the process of cleansing ourselves from the poison and stain of sin and, enkindled by divine fire, hot tears of repentance flow from us, and when our conscience is, as it were, smitten by the heart's anguish, then we experience this acrid feeling and painfulness both spiritually and perceptibly. But when we have been largely cleansed by such tears and have attained freedom from the passions, then—refreshed by the Divine Spirit, our heart pure and tranquil—we are filled with inexpressible tenderness and delight by the joyous tears provoked by compunction.

NIKITAS STITHATOS[24]
IV, ON THE PRACTICE OF THE VIRTUES: ONE HUNDRED TEXTS, SEC. 69

Tears of repentance are one thing, tears that flow because of divine compunction another. The first are like a river in spate that sweeps away all the bastions of sin; the second are to the soul like rain or snow to a field, making it yield a bountiful crop of spiritual knowledge.

NIKITAS STITHATOS
IV, ON THE PRACTICE OF THE VIRTUES: ONE HUNDRED TEXTS, SEC. 70

25 The "desert" is primarily an inner reality rather than a physical location.

+ "This life has been given you for repentance. Do not waste it on other things."

—St. Isaac of Syria, *The Orthodox Way*

I have heard people say that one cannot achieve a persistent state of virtue without retreating far into the desert, and I was amazed that they should think the unconfinable could be confined to a particular locality.... Such a state is not achieved adventitiously, by external influences; it is implanted within us at our creation by virtue of our endemic divine and spiritual consciousness. And when we are impelled by this inner consciousness in accordance with our true nature we are led into the kingdom of heaven, which in our Lord's words, is "within us" (Luke 17:21). Thus the desert is in fact superfluous, since we can enter the kingdom simply through repentance and the strict keeping of God's commandments. Entry into the kingdom can occur, as David states, "in all places of His dominion"; for he says, "In all places of His dominion bless the Lord, O my soul" (Psalm 103:22).[25]

NIKITAS STITHATOS
IV, ON THE PRACTICE OF THE VIRTUES: ONE HUNDRED TEXTS, SEC. 72

When the unbridled water of the intellect's passion-charged thoughts has been bridled through the abiding presence of the Holy Spirit, and the brine-bitter abyss of indecent images and desires has been brought into subjection through self-control and meditation on death, then the divine spirit of repentance begins to blow and the waters of compunction pour forth, and our God and Master, channeling them into the basin of repentance, washes our spiritual feet, making them worthy to walk in the courts of his kingdom.

NIKITAS STITHATOS
IV, ON THE INNER NATURE OF THINGS AND
ON THE PURIFICATION OF THE INTELLECT, SEC. 92

26 Since at least the third century, it has been common for Christian mystics to understand the spiritual journey in three stages—purgative, illuminative, and unitive. These are not necessarily experienced sequentially.

The purgative stage[26] pertains to those newly engaged in spiritual warfare. It is characterized by the rejection of the materialistic self, liberation from material evil, and investiture with the regenerate self, renewed by the Holy Spirit (Colossians 3:10). It involves hatred of materiality, the attenuation of the flesh, the avoidance of whatever incites the mind to passion, repentance for sins committed, the dissolving with tears of the bitter sediment left by sin, the regulation of our life according to the generosity of the Spirit, and the cleansing through compunction of the inside of the cup (Matthew 23:26)—the intellect—from every defilement of flesh and spirit (2 Corinthians 7:1), so that it can then be filled with the wine of the Logos that gladdens the heart of the purified (Psalm 104:15), and can be brought to the King of the celestial powers for him to taste. Its final goal is that we should be forged in the fire of ascetic struggle, scouring off the rust of sin, and steeled and tempered in the water of compunction, so that swordlike we may effectively cut off the passions and the demons. Reaching this point through long ascetic struggle, we quench the fire within us, muzzle the brutelike passions, become strong in the Spirit instead of weak (Hebrews 11:33–34), and like another Job conquer the tempter through our patient endurance.

NIKITAS STITHATOS
IV, ON SPIRITUAL KNOWLEDGE, SEC. 42

27 *Gehenna* is another name for the separation from God, also known
as hell or the place of the departed (Hades). In the Orthodox liturgy
of Pascha (Easter), we are told that Christ looted hell and destroyed
death for all.

Here we should specify the toils and hardships of the ascetic life and explain clearly how we should embark on each task. We must do this lest someone who coasts along without exerting himself, simply relying on what he has heard, and who consequently remains barren, should blame us or other writers, alleging that things are not as we have said. For it is only through travail of heart and bodily toil that the work can be properly carried out. Through them the grace of the Holy Spirit is revealed. This is the grace with which we and all Christians are endowed at baptism but which through neglect of the commandments has been stifled by the passions. Now through God's ineffable mercy it awaits our repentance, so that at the end of our life we may not because of our barrenness hear the words "Take the talent from him" (Matthew 25:28–29), and may not be sent to hell to suffer endlessly in Gehenna.[27] No activity, whether bodily or spiritual, unaccompanied by toil and hardship bears fruit; "for the kingdom of heaven is entered forcibly," says the Lord, "and those who force themselves take possession of it" (Matthew 11:12), where *forcibly* and *force* relate to the body's awareness of exertion in all things.

ST. GREGORY OF SINAI
IV, *ON STILLNESS*, SEC. 14

First the soul has to surmount afflictions embraced willingly, thereby learning to spurn sensual pleasure and self-glory; and this in its turn will permit us readily to bear the afflictions that come unsought. If for the sake of poverty of spirit you spurn each pleasure and self-glory, and also regard yourself as deserving the more drastic remedy of repentance, you will be ready to bear any affliction and will accept any temptation as your due, and you will rejoice when it comes, for you will see it as a cleansing agent for your soul.

ST. GREGORY PALAMAS
IV, *TO THE MOST REVEREND NUN XENIA*, SEC. 46

28 The Fathers of the *Philokalia* want to offer practical advice for making progress in the spiritual life. Here Gregory Palamas makes a point that is elaborated on elsewhere in the *Philokalia*—that sin is best avoided at its inception. The earlier we challenge it in the process of sinning, the more successful we are likely to be in refraining from it.

29 Salvation is synergistic. Our effort is necessary for our salvation, but not sufficient.

But if you are unable to bridle your temper, censure yourself whenever you lose it, and repent before God and before anyone to whom you have spoken or acted evilly. If you repent at the inception of sin you will not commit the sin itself; but if you feel no pang in committing minor offenses you will through them fall into major transgressions.[28]

ST. GREGORY PALAMAS
IV, *A NEW TESTAMENT DECALOGUE,* SEC. 7

Since the Logos of God through his descent to us has brought the kingdom of heaven close to us, let us not distance ourselves from it by leading an unrepentant life.... Let us acquire the fruits of repentance: a humble disposition, compunction and spiritual grief, a gentle and merciful heart that loves righteousness and pursues purity, peaceful, peacemaking, patient in toil, glad to endure persecution, loss, outrage, slander, and suffering for the sake of truth and righteousness. For the kingdom of heaven or, rather, the king of heaven—ineffable in his generosity—is within us (Luke 17:21); and to him we should cleave through acts of repentance and patient endurance, loving as much as we can him who so dearly has loved us.[29]

ST. GREGORY PALAMAS
IV, *TOPICS OF NATURAL AND THEOLOGICAL SCIENCE,* SEC. 57

1   In the *Philokalia,* the *heart* is more than the body's organ that pumps blood. It can refer to the whole person—body, soul, and spirit—or to the spiritual center of the human being.

2   Isaiah (died 491) was a great monk and ascetic who left a text on asceticism, and who represents the genuine spirituality of the Desert Fathers. Nikodimos (the editor of the *Philokalia*) believed Isaiah to have been a contemporary of Makarios in fourth-century Egypt, but the translators of the English edition identify him as a fifth-century monk of Sketis and Palestine.

2 □ The Heart

The demons cunningly withdraw for a time in the hope that we will cease to guard our heart, thinking we have now attained peace; then they suddenly attack our unhappy soul and seize it like a sparrow. Gaining possession of it, they drag it down mercilessly into all kinds of sin, worse than those that we have already committed and for which we have asked forgiveness. Let us stand, therefore, with fear of God and keep guard over our heart, practicing the virtues that check the wickedness of our enemies.[1]

ST. ISAIAH THE SOLITARY
I, *ON GUARDING THE INTELLECT*, SEC. 11

Stand guard, then, over your heart and keep watch on your senses; and if the remembrance of God dwells peaceably within you, you will catch the thieves when they try to deprive you of it. When a man has an exact knowledge about the nature of thoughts, he recognizes those that are about to enter and defile him, troubling the intellect with distractions and making it lazy. Those who recognize these evil thoughts for what they are remain undisturbed and continue in prayer to God.[2]

ST. ISAIAH THE SOLITARY
I, *ON GUARDING THE INTELLECT*, SEC. 12

[+] "For what is prayer? Prayer is the raising of the mind and heart to God—for praise and thanksgiving and beseeching him for the good things necessary for soul and body. The essence of prayer, then, is the mental ascent to God from the heart. The mind stands in the heart consciously before the face of God and, filled with proper and necessary reverence, it begins to pour out its heart before him. This is prayer of the heart! And this should be true of all prayer."

—Theophan the Recluse, *The Duty Also of Those Living in the World*

[3] The traditional morning prayers of the Orthodox Christian include the great penitential Psalm 51 (LXX 50), and the evening prayers continue a daily confession of sins.

I entreat you not to leave your heart unguarded, as long as you are in the body. Just as a farmer cannot feel confident about the crop growing in his fields, because he does not know what will happen to it before it is stored away in his granary, so a man should not leave his heart unguarded as long as he still has breath in his nostrils. Up to his last breath he cannot know what passion will attack him; as long as he breathes, therefore, he must not leave his heart unguarded, but should at every moment pray to God for his help and mercy.

St. Isaiah the Solitary
I, *On Guarding the Intellect*, sec. 15

Once you have begun to seek God with true devotion and with all your heart, then you cannot possibly imagine that you already conform to his will. As long as your conscience reproves you for anything that you have done contrary to nature, you are not set free: the reproof means that you are still under trial and have not yet been acquitted. But if you find when you are praying that nothing at all accuses you, then you are free and by God's will have entered into His peace.

St. Isaiah the Solitary
I, *On Guarding the Intellect*, sec. 18

Examine yourself daily in the sight of God, and discover which of the passions is in your heart. Cast it out, and so escape his judgment.[3]

St. Isaiah the Solitary
I, *On Guarding the Intellect*, sec. 21–22

4 The fasting rules of the Orthodox Church are stricter than the usual Western rules. There are four penitential seasons—the pre-Nativity fast (Advent), the Great Lent, the Apostles' fast (prior to the feast of Peter and Paul on June 29), and the Dormition fast (the two weeks prior to August 15, the feast of the Dormition [falling-asleep] of the Theotokos [the Blessed Virgin Mary]—known in the West as the Assumption). In addition to all the days of these fasting periods, most Wednesdays and Fridays of the year are also fast days. Generally, fasting includes abstinence not only from meat, but also from fish and meat by-products (such as dairy products).

5 John Cassian (ca. 360–435) was probably born in what is now Romania, became a monk in Bethlehem, and then spent about ten years in Egypt as a spiritual son of Evagrios the Solitary. He lived for several years in Constantinople, where he studied under John Chrysostom (ca. 347–407). He spent a few years in Rome before moving to Gaul, where he founded monasteries near Marseilles. He wrote his *Institutes* and *Conferences* in Latin, and they became a great influence on Western monasticism and, in particular, on the *Rule* of St. Benedict (ca. 480–547).

6 John locates sin not in what the eyes see, but in what the heart makes of what the eyes see.

Bodily fasting[4] alone is not enough to bring about self-restraint and true purity; it must be accompanied by contrition of heart, intense prayer to God, frequent meditation on the Scriptures, toil, and manual labor. These are able to check the restless impulses of the soul and to recall it from its shameful fantasies. Humility of soul helps more than anything else, however, and without it no one can overcome unchastity or any other sin. In the first place, then, we must take the utmost care to guard the heart from base thoughts, for, according to the Lord, "Out of the heart proceed evil thoughts, murder, adulteries, unchastity, and so on" (Matthew 15:19).

ST. JOHN CASSIAN[5]
I, ON THE EIGHT VICES

The Doctor of our souls has also placed the remedy in the hidden regions of the soul, recognizing that the cause of our sickness lies there when he says: "Whoever looks at a woman with lust has already committed adultery with her in his heart" (Matthew 5:28). He seeks to correct not so much our inquisitive and unchaste eyes as the soul that has its seat within and makes bad use of the eyes that God gave it for good purposes. That is why the book of Proverbs in its wisdom does not say, "Guard your eyes with all diligence" but "Guard your heart with all diligence" (Proverbs 4:23), imposing the remedy of diligence in the first instance upon that which makes use of the eyes for whatever purpose it desires.[6]

ST. JOHN CASSIAN
I, ON THE EIGHT VICES

7 Mark (early fifth century) was the author of nine works of theology and spirituality, but little else is known about him. He was a monk and hermit, possibly in Palestine, Egypt, or Asia Minor. Perhaps his most important work was *On Holy Baptism.*

8 Mark offers practical counsel by suggesting specific remedies to control specific passions.

To brood on evil makes the heart brazen; but to destroy evil through self-restraint and hope breaks the heart. There is a breaking of the heart that is gentle and makes it deeply penitent, and there is a breaking that is violent and harmful, shattering it completely. Vigils, prayer, and patient acceptance of what comes constitute a breaking that does not harm but benefits the heart, provided we do not destroy the balance between them through excess. He who perseveres in them will be helped in other ways as well; but he who is slack and negligent will suffer intolerably on leaving this life. A self-indulgent heart becomes a prison and chain for the soul when it leaves this life; whereas an assiduous heart is an open door.

ST. MARK THE ASCETIC[7]
I, ON THE SPIRITUAL LAW, SEC. 17–20

If then you wish to conquer these three passions and easily put to flight the hordes of the demonic Philistines, enter within yourself through prayer and with the help of God. Descend into the depths of the heart, and search out these three powerful giants of the devil— forgetfulness, laziness and ignorance, the support of the demonic Philistines—which enable the rest of the evil passions to infiltrate and be active, to live and prevail in the hearts of the self-indulgent and in the souls of the uninstructed. Then through strict attention and control of the intellect, together with help from above, you will track down these evil passions, about which most men are ignorant, not even suspecting their existence, but which are more destructive than all the rest. Take up the weapons of righteousness that are directly opposed to them: mindfulness of God, for this is the cause of all blessings; the light of spiritual knowledge, through which the soul awakens from its slumber and drives out of itself the darkness of ignorance; and true ardor, which makes the soul eager for salvation.[8]

ST. MARK THE ASCETIC
I, LETTER TO NICOLAS THE SOLITARY

9 | Moral judgment has the salutary and practical aim of aiding us in our spiritual warfare. This is not morbid self-flagellation (metaphorical or real); rather, it is analogous to the complete physical examination performed by a physician upon a patient.

Just as someone in the midst of a crowd, holding a mirror and looking at it, sees not only his own face but also the faces of those looking in the mirror with him, so someone who looks into his own heart sees in it not only his own state, but also the black faces of the demons.

ST. HESYCHIOS THE PRIEST
I, ON WATCHFULNESS AND HOLINESS, SEC. 23

The task of moral judgment is always to prompt the soul's incensive power to engage in inner warfare and to make us self-critical. The task of wisdom is to prompt the intelligence to strict watchfulness, constancy, and spiritual contemplation. The task of righteousness is to direct the appetitive aspect of the soul toward holiness and toward God. Fortitude's task is to govern the five senses and to keep them always under control, so that through them neither our inner self, the heart, nor our outer self, the body, is defiled.[9]

ST. HESYCHIOS THE PRIEST
I, ON WATCHFULNESS AND HOLINESS, SEC. 34

Intellect is invisibly interlocked in battle with intellect, the demonic intellect with our own. So from the depths of the heart we must at each instant call on Christ to drive the demonic intellect away from us and in his compassion give us the victory.

ST. HESYCHIOS THE PRIEST
I, ON WATCHFULNESS AND HOLINESS, SEC. 47

10 Here we encounter one of the great spiritual methods of the Fathers of the *Philokalia*—the invocation of the name of Jesus.

11 Hesychios believes that the struggle for obedience is to be fought on the level of the intellect rather than that of the senses. If the intellect is made obedient, the obedience of the senses will not require much effort.

12 This is a reference to the stage of purgation. (See chapter 1, note 26.)

We have learned from experience that for one who wishes to purify the heart it is a truly great blessing constantly to invoke the name of the Lord Jesus against his intelligible enemies. Notice how what I speak of from experience concurs with the testimony of Scripture. It is written: "Prepare yourself, O Israel, to call upon the name of the Lord your God" (Amos 4:12, LXX); and the apostle says: "Pray without ceasing" (1 Thessalonians 5:17). Our Lord himself says: "Without me you can do nothing. If a man dwells in me, and I in him, then he brings forth much fruit"; and again: "If a man does not dwell in me, he is cast out as a branch" (John 15:5–6). Prayer is a great blessing, and it embraces all blessings, for it purifies the heart, in which God is seen by the believer.[10]

ST. HESYCHIOS THE PRIEST
I, *ON WATCHFULNESS AND HOLINESS*, SEC. 62

If a man does not carry out the will and law of God "in his inward parts," that is, in his heart, he will not be able to carry them out easily in the outward sphere of the senses either. The careless and unwatchful man will say to God: "I do not want to know Thy ways" (Job 21:14, LXX),[11] obviously because he lacks divine illumination. But he who participates in that light will be confident and steadfast in matters that concern God.

ST. HESYCHIOS THE PRIEST
I, *ON WATCHFULNESS AND HOLINESS*, SEC. 86

Because every thought enters the heart in the form of a mental image of some sensible object, the blessed light of the Divinity will illumine the heart only when the heart is completely empty of everything and so free from all form. Indeed, this light reveals itself to the pure intellect in the measure to which the intellect is purged of all concepts.[12]

ST. HESYCHIOS THE PRIEST
I, *ON WATCHFULNESS AND HOLINESS*, SEC. 89

13 In historic Christianity, baptism is the beginning of our life in Christ, the mystery (sacrament) of initiation by which we are forgiven our sins and incorporated into Christ.

14 Hesychios reminds us that being a monk is about an inner state more than outward circumstances. A married person living in the world can also be a spiritual athlete; the key is keeping watch on the heart.

The heart that is constantly guarded, and is not allowed to receive the forms, images, and fantasies of the dark and evil spirits, is conditioned by nature to give birth from within itself to thoughts filled with light. For just as coal engenders a flame, or a flame lights a candle, so will God, who from our baptism dwells in our heart, kindle our mind to contemplation when he finds it free from the winds of evil and protected by the guarding of the intellect.[13]

ST. HESYCHIOS THE PRIEST
I, ON WATCHFULNESS AND HOLINESS, SEC. 104

A heart that has been completely emptied of mental images gives birth to divine, mysterious intellections that sport within like fish and dolphins in a calm sea. The sea is fanned by a soft wind, the heart's depth by the Holy Spirit. "And because you are sons, God has sent forth the spirit of his Son into your hearts, crying: 'Abba, Father'" (Galatians 4:6).

ST. HESYCHIOS THE PRIEST
I, ON WATCHFULNESS AND HOLINESS, SEC. 156

A true monk is one who has achieved watchfulness; and he who is truly watchful is a monk in his heart.[14]

ST. HESYCHIOS THE PRIEST
I, ON WATCHFULNESS AND HOLINESS, SEC. 159

15 Diadochos (ca. 400–485) was bishop of Photiki in northern Greece. He is remembered for his *On Spiritual Knowledge and Discrimination,* which is an important text for the mystical theology of the Orthodox Church. His work shows the influence of Evagrios the Solitary, but he emphasizes some important aspects of the spiritual life that are not treated by Evagrios—the prayer of Jesus, the mysteries (sacraments), and the importance of love.

16 Although Diadochos here speaks of invoking the name of Jesus, he ties it to obedience to God's commandments.

Eve is the first to teach us that sight, taste, and the other senses, when used without moderation, distract the heart from its remembrance of God. As long as she did not look with longing at the forbidden tree, she was able to keep God's commandment carefully in mind; she was still covered by the wings of divine love and thus was ignorant of her own nakedness.... We should therefore always be looking into the depths of our heart with continued remembrance of God, and should pass through this deceitful life like men who have lost their sight. It is the mark of true spiritual wisdom always to clip the wings of our love for visible appearances, and this is what Job, in his great experience, refers to when he says: "If my heart has followed my eye ... " (Job 31:7, LXX). To master ourselves in this way is evidence of the greatest self-control.

ST. DIADOCHOS OF PHOTIKI[15]
I, ON SPIRITUAL KNOWLEDGE AND DISCRIMINATION, SEC. 56

The reason that we have both good and wicked thoughts together is not, as some suppose, because the Holy Spirit and the devil dwell together in our intellect, but because we have not yet consciously experienced the goodness of the Lord. As I have said before, grace at first conceals its presence in those who have been baptized, waiting to see which way the soul inclines; but when the whole man has turned toward the Lord, it then reveals to the heart its presence there with a feeling that words cannot express, once again waiting to see which way the soul inclines. At the same time, however, it allows the arrows of the devil to wound the soul at the most inward part of its sensitivity, so as to make the soul search out God with warmer resolve and more humble disposition. If, then, a man begins to make progress in keeping the commandments and calls ceaselessly upon the Lord Jesus, the fire of God's grace spreads even to the heart's more outward organs of perception, consciously burning up the tares in the field of the soul.[16]

ST. DIADOCHOS OF PHOTIKI
I, ON SPIRITUAL KNOWLEDGE AND DISCRIMINATION, SEC. 85

17 John of Karpathos (ca. seventh century) was an ascetic who left two texts encouraging monastics who were thinking of abandoning the religious life. Nothing else about him is certain—he may have been from the Mediterranean island of Karpathos or the Bishop John of an island called Karpathion. The editors of the English *Philokalia* say that the monks "in India" to whom he wrote may actually have been in Ethiopia.

While the intellect tries to think continually of what is good, it suddenly recollects what is bad, since from the time of Adam's disobedience man's power of thinking has been split into two modes. But when we begin wholeheartedly to carry out the commandments of God, all our organs of perception will become fully conscious of the light of grace; grace will consume our thoughts with its flames, sweetening our hearts in the peace of uninterrupted love, and enabling us to think spiritual thoughts and no longer worldly thoughts. These effects of grace are always present in those who are approaching perfection and have the remembrance of the Lord Jesus unceasingly in their hearts.

ST. DIADOCHOS OF PHOTIKI
I, *ON SPIRITUAL KNOWLEDGE AND DISCRIMINATION*, SEC. 88

So as not to be deceived and carried away by the vain and empty things that the senses bring before us, we should listen to the words of the prophet Isaiah: "Come, my people, enter into your inner room" (26:20)—the shrine of your heart, which is closed to every conception derived from the sensible world, that image-free dwelling place illumined by dispassion and the overshadowing of God's grace.... A man escapes [the Lord's] anger by keeping his attention fixed continually within his heart during prayer, and by striving to remain within his inner sanctuary.

ST. JOHN OF KARPATHOS[17]
I, *FOR THE ENCOURAGEMENT OF THE MONKS IN INDIA*, SEC. 91

18 Theodoros (ninth century?) is named by Nikodimos as the author of two texts in the *Philokalia*. Theodoros belonged to the monastery of Sabas, which is located near Jerusalem. He was later to become a bishop of Edessa.

One of the ancients spoke wisely and simply about thoughts. Judge thoughts, he said, before the judgment seat of the heart, to discern whether they are ours or those of our enemy. Place those that are good and properly our own in the inmost shrine of the soul, keeping them in this inviolable treasury. But chastise hostile thoughts with the whip of the intelligence and banish them, giving them no place, no abode within the bounds of your soul. Or, to speak more fittingly, slay them completely with the sword of prayer and divine meditation, so that when the robbers have been destroyed, their chief may take fright. For, as he says, a man who examines his thoughts strictly is one who also truly loves the commandments.

ST. THEODOROS THE GREAT ASCETIC[18]
II, *A CENTURY OF SPIRITUAL TEXTS*, SEC. 70

If a man's heart does not condemn him (1 John 3:21) for having rejected a commandment of God, or for negligence, or for accepting a hostile thought, then he is pure of heart and worthy to have Christ say to him, "Blessed are the pure in heart, for they shall see God" (Matthew 5:8).

ST. THEODOROS THE GREAT ASCETIC
II, *A CENTURY OF SPIRITUAL TEXTS*, SEC. 86

If, as St. Paul says, Christ dwells in our hearts through faith (Ephesians 3:17), and all the treasures of wisdom and spiritual knowledge are hidden in him (Colossians 2:3), then all the treasures of wisdom and spiritual knowledge are hidden in our hearts. They are revealed to the heart in proportion to our purification by means of the commandments.

ST. MAXIMOS THE CONFESSOR
II, *FOURTH CENTURY ON LOVE*, SEC. 70

19 In the Russian version of the Divine Liturgy (Eucharist), the Beatitudes are sung on most Sundays of the year, a constant reminder that they describe the life Christians are called to live in the present.

20 In the Orthodox spiritual tradition, a good deal is made of the Transfiguration of Christ and the light of the Transfiguration on Mount Tabor. First, Orthodoxy sees the Transfiguration as the destiny of all creation, that is, the entire universe is to be transfigured with the glory of God. Second, the experience of *theosis* on Mount Athos has often been described as a participation in the "Taboric light."

21 Here Maximos picks up the prophecy of Jeremiah 31, which speaks of the time when God will write his laws in the hearts of the people.

It is for this reason that the Savior says, "Blessed are the pure in heart, for they shall see God" (Matthew 5:8): for he is hidden in the hearts of those who believe in him. They shall see him and the riches that are in him when they have purified themselves through love and self-control; and the greater their purity, the more they will see.[19]

ST. MAXIMOS THE CONFESSOR
II, *FOURTH CENTURY ON LOVE*, SEC. 72

Circumcision of the heart in the spirit signifies the utter stripping away from the senses and the intellect of their natural activities connected with sensible and intelligible things. This stripping away is accomplished by the Spirit's immediate presence, which completely transfigures body and soul and makes them more divine.[20]

ST. MAXIMOS THE CONFESSOR
II, *FIRST CENTURY ON THEOLOGY*, SEC. 46

He who has made his heart pure will not only know the inner essences of what is sequent to God and dependent on him but, after passing through all of them, he will in some measure see God himself, which is the supreme consummation of all blessings. When God comes to dwell in such a heart, he honors it by engraving his own letters on it through the Holy Spirit, just as he did on the Mosaic tablets (Exodus 31:18). This he does according to the degree to which the heart, through the practice of the virtues and contemplation, has devoted itself to the admonition that bids us, in a mystical sense, "Be fruitful and multiply" (Genesis 35:11). A pure heart is perhaps one that has no natural propulsion toward anything in any manner whatsoever. When in its extreme simplicity such a heart has become like a writing tablet beautifully smoothed and polished, God comes to dwell in it and writes there his own laws.[21] A pure heart is one that offers the mind to God free of all image and form, and ready to be imprinted only with his own archetypes, by which God himself is made manifest.

ST. MAXIMOS THE CONFESSOR
II, *SECOND CENTURY ON THEOLOGY*, SEC. 80–82

22 Philotheos (ninth or tenth century?) clearly belongs to the spiritual tradition of St. Catherine's Monastery on Mount Sinai, but we cannot be sure exactly when he lived. His *Forty Texts on Watchfulness* is an important summary of the importance of watchfulness (*nepsis*). The importance of this theme may be seen in the full title of the collection— *The Philokalia of the Neptic Fathers.* The watchfulness he writes of is primarily over the *nous*, that faculty of the human soul whereby we experience the knowledge of God. The monk must struggle to purify the *nous* from sin and to keep it free from sin in the future.

Love and genuine affection—that is, faith and a clear conscience—are clearly the result of a hidden impulse of the heart; for the heart is fully able to generate without using external matter.

ST. MAXIMOS THE CONFESSOR
II, *FOURTH CENTURY OF VARIOUS TEXTS*, SEC. 61

There is within us, on the noetic plane, a warfare tougher than that on the plane of the senses. The spiritual worker has to press on with his intellect toward the goal (Philippians 3:14), in order to enshrine perfectly the remembrance of God in his heart like some pearl or precious stone (Matthew 13:44–46). He has to give up everything, including the body, and to disdain this present life, if he wishes to possess God alone in his heart. For the noetic vision of God, the divine Chrysostom has said, can by itself destroy the demonic spirits.

ST. PHILOTHEOS OF SINAI[22]
III, *FORTY TEXTS ON WATCHFULNESS*, SEC. 1

Where humility is combined with the remembrance of God that is established through watchfulness and attention, and also with recurrent prayer inflexible in its resistance to the enemy, there is the place of God, the heaven of the heart in which because of God's presence no demonic army dares to make a stand.

ST. PHILOTHEOS OF SINAI
III, *FORTY TEXTS ON WATCHFULNESS*, SEC. 4

+ "When you feel the touch of the Eternal Spirit in your heart ... love streams like a light on all creation. Though the physical heart feels this love, in kind it is spiritual—metaphysical.... Yet only those ... who keep a clear conscience not only before God but towards their neighbor, towards animals—even towards the material things which are the product of men's labor—will care for all creation.... [Love] embraces all created beings in joy over their salvation.... For the Divine Spirit draws the heart to compassion for all creation."

—Sophrony of Essex, *Light through Darkness:*
The Orthodox Tradition

Once we have in some measure acquired the habit of self-control, and have learned how to shun visible sins brought about through the five senses, we will then be able to guard the heart with Jesus, to receive his illumination within it, and by means of the intellect to taste his goodness with a certain ardent longing. For we have been commanded to purify the heart precisely so that, through dispelling the clouds of evil from it by continual attentiveness, we may perceive the sun of righteousness, Jesus, as though in clear sky; and so that the principles of His majesty may shine to some extent in the intellect. For these principles are revealed only to those who purify their minds.

ST. PHILOTHEOS OF SINAI
III, *FORTY TEXTS ON WATCHFULNESS*, SEC. 8

+ "At last, I was completely changed, and forgot myself. I was filled with light in my heart and outside and everywhere, not being aware that I even had a body. The 'prayer' [that is, the Jesus Prayer] began to say itself within me so rhythmically that I was amazed, since I myself was not making any effort."

—Elder Joseph the Hesychast,
Light through Darkness: The Orthodox Tradition

23 As in the rabbinical tradition of Judaism, anger is understood as a serious sin that is the doorway to murder.

Note how Christ says, "Whoever is angry with his brother without good cause will be brought to judgment" (Matthew 5:22), and then tells us how anger may be healed. But the enemy in his turn tries to subvert this commandment by stirring up strife and thoughts of rancor and envy within us. For he too knows that the intelligence should control the incensive power; and so, by bombarding the intelligence with evil thoughts—with thoughts of envy, strife, contention, guile, self-esteem—he persuades the intelligence to abandon its control, to hand the reins over to the incensive power, and to let the latter go unchecked. And the incensive power, having, so to speak, unseated its rider, disgorges through the mouth in the form of words all those things stored up in the heart as a result of the devil's wiles and the intellect's negligence. And the heart is then seen to be full, not of the Divine Spirit and of godlike spirits, but of evil. It is as the Lord said: "The mouth expresses what fills the heart" (Matthew 12:34). For if the devil can induce the person he has taken possession of to utter what is harbored within, then that person will not merely call his brother "dolt" or "fool" but may well pass from insulting words to murder. It is in these ways that the devil fights against God and the commandment God gave about not being angry with one's brother without good cause. But the insulting words and their consequences could have been avoided had their initial provocations been expelled from the heart through prayer and attentiveness. Thus the devil achieves his purpose when he makes us break God's commandment by means of the thoughts that he insinuates into the heart.[23]

ST. PHILOTHEOS OF SINAI
III, *FORTY TEXTS ON WATCHFULNESS*, SEC. 16

24 The spiritual struggle is primarily an inner one, for the kingdom of God—indeed, God himself—dwells within us.

25 The mindfulness of death is a constant monastic theme. In this passage, Philotheos gives several reasons why this is so.

26 The Psalms are the heart of the common prayer of the Church's divine office—the formal services of prayer throughout the day that are observed primarily in monasteries.

At every hour and moment let us guard the heart with all diligence
from thoughts that obscure the soul's mirror; for in that mirror Jesus
Christ, the wisdom and power of God the Father (1 Corinthians 1:24),
is typified and luminously reflected. And let us unceasingly seek the
kingdom of heaven inside our heart (Luke 17:21), the seed (Luke
13:19), the pearl (Matthew 13:45), and the leaven (Matthew 13:33).
Indeed, if we cleanse the eye of the intellect, we will find all things
hidden within us. This is why our Lord Jesus Christ said that the
kingdom of heaven is within us, indicating that the Divinity dwells in
our hearts.[24]

St. Philotheos of Sinai
III, *Forty Texts on Watchfulness*, sec. 23

Vivid mindfulness of death embraces many virtues. It begets grief; it
promotes the exercise of self-control in all things; it is a reminder of
hell; it is the mother of prayer and tears; it induces guarding of the
heart and detachment from material things; it is a source of
attentiveness and discrimination. These in their turn produce the
twofold fear of God. In addition, the purging of impassioned thoughts
from the heart embraces many of the Lord's commandments. The
harsh hour-by-hour struggle, in which so many athletes of Christ are
engaged, has as its aim precisely this purging of the heart.[25]

St. Philotheos of Sinai
III, *Forty Texts on Watchfulness*, sec. 38

When through continuous prayer the words of the Psalms are brought
down into the heart, then the heart like good soil begins to produce
by itself various flowers: roses, the vision of incorporeal realities; lilies,
the luminosity of corporeal realities; and violets, the many judgments
of God, hard to understand.[26]

Ilias the Presbyter
III, *Gnomic Anthology IV*, sec. 78

27 Makarios of Egypt (ca. 300–390), also known as "Makarios the Great," was one of the original Desert Fathers, and he founded the monastery at Sketis in 360, which is still in operation. (The particular desert was known as Nitria, but is now known as Wadi Natrun.) Makarios was well known in his day for his great asceticism and extraordinary charismatic gifts.

"Cleanse me from my secret faults," writes the psalmist (Psalm 19:12), as though to say that through much prayer and faith, and by turning completely to God, we are able, with the help of the Spirit, to conquer them. But this on condition that we too strive against them and keep strict watch over our heart (Proverbs 4:23).

ST. MAKARIOS OF EGYPT[27]

III, *SPIRITUAL PERFECTION*, SEC. 3

For truly the heart is an immeasurable abyss. If you have destroyed that serpent, have cleansed yourself of all inner lawlessness, and have expelled sin, you may boast to God of your purity; but if not, you should humble yourself because you are still a sinner and in need, and ask Christ to come to you on account of your secret sins. The whole Old and New Testaments speaks of purity, and everyone, whether Jew or Greek, should long for purity even though not all can attain it. Purity of heart can be brought about only by Jesus; for he is authentic and absolute truth, and without this truth it is impossible to know the truth or to achieve salvation.

ST. MAKARIOS OF EGYPT

III, *THE RAISING OF THE INTELLECT*, SEC. 83

When you hear that Christ descended into hell in order to deliver the souls dwelling there, do not think that what happens now is very different. The heart is a tomb and there our thoughts and our intellect are buried, imprisoned in heavy darkness. And so Christ comes to the souls in hell that call upon him, descending, that is to say, into the depths of the heart; and there he commands death to release the imprisoned souls that call upon him, for he has power to deliver us. Then, lifting up the heavy stone that oppresses the soul, and opening the tomb, he resurrects us—for we were truly dead—and releases our imprisoned soul from its lightless prison.

ST. MAKARIOS OF EGYPT

III, *THE FREEDOM OF THE INTELLECT*, SEC. 116

28 When they read biblical passages such as Paul's claim in Romans that nothing can separate us from the love of Christ, many Christians may believe what they read but do not know its truth deep in their heart. Symeon explains that being able to savor such a truth is the fruit of "true and unerring attentiveness and prayer."

29 Such clairvoyance is understood to be part of the gift of the discernment of spirits, often possessed by spiritual elders.

True and unerring attentiveness and prayer mean that the intellect
keeps watch over the heart while it prays; it should always be on
patrol within the heart, and from within—from the depths of the
heart—it should offer up prayers to God. Once it has tasted within the
heart that the Lord is bountiful (Psalm 34:8, LXX), then the intellect
will have no desire to leave the heart, and it will repeat the words of
the apostle Peter, "It is good for us to be here" (Matthew 17:4). It will
keep watch always within the heart, repulsing and expelling all
thoughts sown there by the enemy. To those who have no knowledge
of this practice, it appears extremely harsh and arduous; and indeed it
is oppressive and laborious, not only to the uninitiated, but also to
those who, although genuinely experienced, have not yet felt the
delight to be found in the depths of the heart. But those who have
savored this delight proclaim with St. Paul, "Who will separate us from
the love of Christ?" (Romans 8:35).**28**

ST. SYMEON THE NEW THEOLOGIAN
IV, *THE THREE METHODS OF PRAYER*

A good spring does not produce turbid, foul-smelling water, redolent
of worldly matter; nor can a heart that is outside the kingdom of
heaven gush with streams of divine life, giving out the sweet savor of
spiritual myrrh.

NIKITAS STITHATOS
IV, *ON THE PRACTICE OF THE VIRTUES: ONE HUNDRED TEXTS*, SEC. 99

Do you see how, through watchfulness of the heart, St. Antony was
able to perceive God and to acquire the power of clairvoyance?**29** For
it is in the heart that God manifests himself to the intellect, first—
according to St. John Klimakos—as fire that purifies the lover and
then as light that illumines the intellect and renders it godlike.

NIKIPHOROS THE MONK
IV, *ON WATCHFULNESS AND THE GUARDING OF THE HEART*

30   As mentioned earlier with respect to prostrations, outward effort
(in this case, chastity) is worthless unless it is an expression of an inner
reality.

+   "Within the heart are unfathomable depths. It is but a small vessel:
and yet dragons and lions are there, and there poisonous creatures
and all the treasures of wickedness; rough, uneven paths are there, and
gaping chasms. There likewise is God, there are the angels, there life
and the Kingdom, there light and the Apostles, the heavenly cities and
the treasures of grace: all things are there."

—"The Homilies of St Macarius," *The Orthodox Way,*

The most important task for an ascetic is to enter into his heart, to wage war against satan, to hate him, and to battle with him by wrestling against the thoughts he provokes. If you keep your body outwardly chaste and pure, but inwardly are adulterous where God is concerned and profligate in your thoughts, then you gain nothing from keeping your body chaste.[30]

NIKIPHOROS THE MONK
IV, ON WATCHFULNESS AND THE GUARDING OF THE HEART

A true sanctuary, even before the life to come, is a heart free from distractive thoughts and energized by the Spirit, for all is done and said there spiritually. If we do not attain such a state in this life, we may because of our other virtues be a stone fit for building into the temple of God; but we will not ourselves be a temple or a celebrant of the Spirit.

ST. GREGORY OF SINAI
IV, ON COMMANDMENTS AND DOCTRINES, SEC. 7

31　An important Desert Father of sixth-century Palestine.

32　The Hours are the offices of common prayer.

33　The Trisagion ("Thrice-Holy") is a regular component of the Divine Liturgy, the Hours, and the individual prayers of the Orthodox Christian. The text of the prayer is: "Holy God, Holy Mighty, Holy Immortal, have mercy on us."

"When the watchman grows weary," says St. John Klimakos, "he stands up and prays; then he sits down again and courageously resumes the same task." Although St. John is here referring to the intellect and is saying that it should behave in this matter when it has learned how to guard the heart, yet what he says can apply equally to psalmody. For it is said that when the great Varsanuphios[31] was asked about how one should psalmodize, he replied, 'The Hours[32] and the liturgical Odes are church traditions, rightly given so that concord is maintained when there are many praying together. But the monks of Sketis do not recite the Hours, nor do they sing Odes. On their own they practice manual labor, meditation, and a little prayer. When you stand in prayer, you should repeat the Trisagion[33] and the Lord's Prayer. You should also ask God to deliver you from your fallen selfhood. Do not grow slack in doing this; your mind should be concentrated in prayer all day long." What St. Varsanuphios wanted to make clear is that private meditation is the prayer of the heart, and that to practice "a little prayer" means to stand and psalmodize. Moreover, St. John Klimakos explicitly says that to attain the state of stillness entails first total detachment; second, resolute prayer—this means standing and psalmodizing—and third, unbroken labor of the heart, that is to say, sitting down to pray in stillness.

St. Gregory of Sinai
IV, On Stillness, sec. 4

Since our soul is a single entity possessing many powers, it utilizes as an organ the body that by nature lives in conjunction with it. What organs, then, does the power of the soul that we call *intellect* make use of when it is active? No one has ever supposed that the mind resides in the fingernails or the eyelashes, the nostrils or the lips. But we all agree that it resides within us, even though we may not all agree as to which of our own inner organs it chiefly makes use of. For some locate it in

(continued on page 69)

34 Gregory Palamas indicates that the "heart," understood as the spiritual center of the person, is not simply equivalent to the physical organ that goes by the same name, even though they are associated.

35 Gregory Palamas (1296–1359) was a monk of Mount Athos who became archbishop of Thessalonica in 1347, and his importance is signified by the Orthodox Church's tradition of commemorating him on the Second Sunday of Lent. His best-known work, *The Triads in Defense of the Holy Hesychasts,* articulated traditional hesychastic teaching on *theosis* ("deification"), the distinction between God's essence and God's energies, and our direct experience of God through participation in those energies.

the head, as though in a sort of acropolis; others consider that its
vehicle is the centermost part of the heart, that aspect of the heart that
has been purified from natural life. We know very well that our
intelligence is neither within us as in a container—for it is
incorporeal—nor yet outside us, for it is united to us; but it is located
in the heart as in its own organ.[34] And we know this because we are
taught it not by men but by the Creator of man himself when he says,
"It is not that which goes into man's mouth that defiles him, but what
comes out of it" (Matthew 15:11), adding, "for thoughts come out of
the heart" (Matthew 15:19). St. Makarios the Great says the same:
"The heart rules over the whole human organism, and when grace
takes possession of the pastures of the heart, it reigns over all a man's
thoughts and members. For the intellect and all the thoughts of the
soul are located there."

Our heart is, therefore, the shrine of the intelligence and the chief
intellectual organ of the body. When, therefore, we strive to scrutinize
and to amend our intelligence through rigorous watchfulness, how
could we do this if we did not collect our intellect, outwardly
dispersed through the senses, and bring it back within ourselves—back
to the heart itself, the shrine of the thoughts? It is for this reason that
St. Makarios—rightly called blessed—directly after what he says
above, adds: "So it is there that we must look to see whether grace has
inscribed the laws of the Spirit." Where? In the ruling organ, in the
throne of grace, where the intellect and all the thoughts of the soul
reside, that is to say, in the heart. Do you see, then, how greatly
necessary it is for those who have chosen a life of self-attentiveness
and stillness to bring their intellect back and to enclose it within their
body, and particularly within that innermost body within the body
that we call the heart?

ST. GREGORY PALAMAS[35]

IV, *IN DEFENSE OF THOSE WHO PRACTICE A LIFE OF STILLNESS*, SEC. 3

1 Evagrios the Solitary (346–399), also known as Evagrios of Pontus, was a monk and an ascetic. His spiritual father was Makarios of Alexandria (died ca. 395), and he also knew Makarios of Egypt. He was ordained reader by Basil the Great (ca. 330–379) and deacon by his friend and mentor, Gregory of Nazianzus (329–389), known in the East as Gregory the Theologian. He was greatly influenced by the Cappadocians—Basil the Great, Gregory of Nyssa (ca. 340–394), Gregory of Nazianzus, and Macrina (ca. 330–380)—and by Origen (ca. 175–254). His works, written in Greek and subsequently translated into Syriac and Latin, were very influential in shaping the Eastern spiritual tradition.

2 Obedience to God's commandments is the first step in the spiritual life.

3 □ Prayer

If you are disheartened, pray, as the apostle says (James 5:13). Pray with fear, trembling, effort, with inner watchfulness and vigilance. To pray in this manner is especially necessary because the enemies are so malignant. For it is just when they see us at prayer that they come and stand beside us, ready to attack, suggesting to our intellect the very things we should not think about when praying; in this way they try to take our intellect captive and to make our prayer and supplication vain and useless. For prayer is truly vain and useless when not performed with fear and trembling, with inner watchfulness and vigilance.

EVAGRIOS THE SOLITARY[1]
I, OUTLINE TEACHING ON ASCETICISM AND
STILLNESS IN THE SOLITARY LIFE

When the soul has been purified through the keeping of all the commandments, it makes the intellect steadfast and able to receive the state needed for prayer. Prayer is the communion of the intellect with God.[2]

EVAGRIOS THE SOLITARY
I, ON PRAYER, SEC. 2–3

3 John Chrysostom is thinking along these lines when he writes, "The mystery [of the Eucharist] requires that we should be innocent not only of violence but of all enmity, however slight, for it is the mystery of peace."

If you desire to pray as you ought, do not grieve anyone; otherwise you "run in vain" (Philippians 2:16). "Leave your gift before the altar; first go away and be reconciled with your brother" (Matthew 5:24), and when you return you will pray without disturbance. For rancor darkens the intellect of one who prays, and extinguishes the light of his prayers.[3]

EVAGRIOS THE SOLITARY
I, *ON PRAYER*, SEC. 21–22

Undistracted prayer is the highest intellection of the intellect. Prayer is the ascent of the intellect to God. If you long for prayer, renounce all to gain all. Pray first for the purification of the passions; second, for deliverance from ignorance and forgetfulness; and third, for deliverance from all temptation, trial, and dereliction.

EVAGRIOS THE SOLITARY
I, *ON PRAYER*, SEC. 35–38

Do not pray only with outward forms and gestures, but with reverence and awe try to make your intellect conscious of spiritual prayer.

EVAGRIOS THE SOLITARY
I, *ON PRAYER*, SEC. 28

4 Buddhists refer to this distraction from prayer as "monkey mind"—when we try to still the mind, it seems determined to "jump from tree to tree," that is, from thought to thought.

5 For the Church Fathers in the Eastern Christian tradition, *theology* refers first to God the Trinity; second to the experience of God the Trinity; third to the worship of God the Trinity; fourth to the Holy Scriptures; and last (and arguably least) to "thinking about God."

If your intellect is still distracted during prayer, you do not yet know what it is to pray as a monk; but your prayer is still worldly, embellishing the outer tabernacle. When you pray, keep close watch on your memory, so that it does not distract you with recollections of your past. But make yourself aware that you are standing before God. For by nature the intellect is apt to be carried away by memories during prayer. While you are praying, the memory brings before you fantasies either of past things, or of recent concerns, or of the face of someone who has irritated you. The demon is very envious of us when we pray, and uses every kind of trick to thwart our purpose. Therefore he is always using our memory to stir up thoughts of various things and our flesh to arouse our passions, in order to obstruct our way of ascent to God.[4]

EVAGRIOS THE SOLITARY
I, ON PRAYER, SEC. 45–47

The state of prayer is one of dispassion, which by virtue of the most intense love transports to the noetic realm the intellect that longs for wisdom.

EVAGRIOS THE SOLITARY
I, ON PRAYER, SEC. 53

He who prays in spirit and in truth is no longer dependent on created things when honoring the Creator, but praises him for and in himself.

EVAGRIOS THE SOLITARY
I, ON PRAYER, SEC. 60

If you are a theologian, you will pray truly. And if you pray truly, you are a theologian.[5]

EVAGRIOS THE SOLITARY
I, ON PRAYER, SEC. 61

6 Hesychios the Priest (eighth or ninth century) was thought by Nikodimos to have been the early fifth-century Hesychios of Jerusalem, but nowadays he is believed to have been the later Hesychios, who was abbot of a monastery on Sinai. His work draws on Maximos Confessor, Mark the Ascetic, and John Klimakos (ca. 579–649). He emphasized devotion to the name of Jesus.

7 Unceasing prayer first brings us to the stage of purgation, which is naturally followed by the second stage of illumination. But Hesychios warns that a lack of humility will prevent this illumination.

I shall say again what I have said elsewhere: blessed is the intellect that is completely free from forms during prayer. Blessed is the intellect that, undistracted in its prayer, acquires an even greater longing for God. Blessed is the intellect that during prayer is free from materiality and stripped of all possessions. Blessed is the intellect that has acquired complete freedom from sensations during prayer.

EVAGRIOS THE SOLITARY
I, ON PRAYER, SEC. 117–120

If we have not attained prayer that is free from thoughts, we have no weapon to fight with. By this prayer I mean the prayer that is ever active in the inner shrine of the soul, and that, by invoking Christ, scourges and sears our enemy.

ST. HESYCHIOS THE PRIEST[6]
I, ON WATCHFULNESS AND HOLINESS, SEC. 21

It is written: "Prepare yourself, O Israel, to call upon the name of the Lord your God" (Amos 4:12, LXX); and the apostle says, "Pray without ceasing" (1 Thessalonians 5:17). Our Lord himself says, "Without me you can do nothing. If a man dwells in me and I in him, then he brings forth much fruit"; and again: "If a man does not dwell in me, he is cast out as a branch" (John 15:5–6). Prayer is a great blessing, and it embraces all blessings, for it purifies the heart, in which God is seen by the believer.

ST. HESYCHIOS THE PRIEST
I, ON WATCHFULNESS AND HOLINESS, SEC. 62

It is through unceasing prayer that the mind is cleansed of the dark clouds, the tempests of the demons. And when it is cleansed, the divine light of Jesus cannot but shine in it, unless we are puffed up by self-esteem and delusion and a love of ostentation, and elevate ourselves toward the unattainable, and so are deprived of Jesus's help. For Christ, the paradigm of humility, loathes all such self-inflation.[7]

ST. HESYCHIOS THE PRIEST
I, ON WATCHFULNESS AND HOLINESS, SEC. 175

8 Prayer, like faith itself, is a gift from God. But we must actively accept the gift through our participation.

The Fathers define prayer as a spiritual weapon. Unless we are armed with it, we cannot engage in warfare, but are carried off as prisoners to the enemy's country. Nor can we acquire pure prayer unless we cleave to God with an upright heart. For it is God who gives prayer to him who prays and who teaches man spiritual knowledge.[8]

ST. THEODOROS THE GREAT ASCETIC
II, *A CENTURY OF SPIRITUAL TEXTS,* SEC. 8

Especially important is pure prayer—prayer that is unceasing and uninterrupted. Such prayer is a safe fortress, a sheltered harbor, a protector of virtues, a destroyer of passions. It brings vigor to the soul, purifies the intellect, gives rest to those who suffer, consoles those who mourn. Prayer is converse with God, contemplation of the invisible, the angelic mode of life, a stimulus toward the Divine, the assurance of things longed for, "making real the things for which we hope" (Hebrews 11:1). As an ascetic you must embrace this queen of the virtues with all your strength. Pray day and night. Pray at times of dejection and at times of exhilaration. Pray with fear and trembling, with a watchful and vigilant mind, so that prayer may be accepted by the Lord. For, as the psalmist says: "The eyes of the Lord are on the righteous and his ears are open to their prayer" (Psalm 34:15).

ST. THEODOROS THE GREAT ASCETIC
II, *A CENTURY OF SPIRITUAL TEXTS,* SEC. 60

9 The monastic tradition emphasizes the importance of rising early to praise God.

10 In the West, there is a strong tradition of prayer using images (*kataphatic* prayer), as well as imageless (*apophatic*) prayer. In the East, however, and especially in the Athonite (that is, having to do with Mount Athos) spirituality contained in the *Philokalia,* the use of images in prayer is strongly discouraged.

Whatever a man loves, he desires at all costs to be near to continuously and uninterruptedly, and he turns himself away from everything that hinders him from being in contact and dwelling with the object of his love. It is clear therefore that he who loves God also desires always to be with him and to converse with him. This comes to pass in us through pure prayer. Accordingly, let us apply ourselves to prayer with all our power; for it enables us to become akin to God. Such a man was he who said: "O God, my God, I cry to Thee at dawn; my soul has thirsted for Thee" (Psalm 63:1, LXX). For the man who cries to God at dawn has withdrawn his intellect from every vice and clearly is wounded by divine love.[9]

ST. THEODOROS THE GREAT ASCETIC
II, *A CENTURY OF SPIRITUAL TEXTS,* SEC. 94

Prayer gives thanks for blessings received and asks for failures to be forgiven and for power to strengthen us for the future; for without God's help the soul can indeed do nothing. Nonetheless, to persuade the will to have the strongest possible desire for union with and enjoyment of God, for whom it longs, and to direct itself totally toward him, is the major part of the achievement of our aim.

ST. THEODOROS THE GREAT ASCETIC
II, *THEORETIKON*

Almsgiving heals the soul's incensive power; fasting withers sensual desire; prayer purifies the intellect and prepares it for the contemplation of created things. For the Lord has given us commandments that correspond to the powers of the soul.

ST. MAXIMOS THE CONFESSOR
II, *FIRST CENTURY ON LOVE,* SEC. 79

When during prayer no conceptual image of anything worldly disturbs your intellect, then know that you are within the realm of dispassion.[10]

ST. MAXIMOS THE CONFESSOR
II, *FIRST CENTURY ON LOVE,* SEC. 88

+ "Christ becomes king over man's soul through man's frequent prayer and the outpouring of his self. He becomes the true center of its being and movements. At that stage, man will never find rest in anything except in Christ alone, where the image would rest in its own likeness. Since the soul has been created for immortality, it will thus find in Christ, when it unites with him, its ultimate joy. Through his existence, he consummates its own existence and immortality."

—Matthew the Poor, *Orthodox Prayer Life: The Inner Way*

11 Imageless prayer is seen as superior to the use of images in prayer, and as necessary to unceasing prayer.

He who truly loves God prays entirely without distraction, and he
who prays entirely without distraction loves God truly. But he whose
intellect is fixed on any worldly thing does not pray without
distraction, and consequently he does not love God.

St. Maximos the Confessor
II, *Second Century on Love*, sec. 1

Two states of pure prayer are exalted above all others. One is to be
found in those who have not advanced beyond the practice of the
virtues, the other in those leading the contemplative life. The first is
engendered in the soul by fear of God and a firm hope in him, the
second by an intense longing for God and by total purification. The
sign of the first is that the intellect, abandoning all conceptual images
of the world, concentrates itself and prays without distraction or
disturbance as if God himself were present, as indeed he is. The sign
of the second is that at the very onset of prayer the intellect is so
ravished by the divine and infinite light that it is aware neither of itself
nor of any other created thing, but only of him who through love has
activated such radiance in it. It is then that, being made aware of God's
qualities, it receives clear and distinct reflections of him.

St. Maximos the Confessor
II, *Second Century on Love*, sec. 6

It is said that the highest state of prayer is reached when the intellect
goes beyond the flesh and the world, and while praying is utterly free
from matter and form. He who maintains this state has truly attained
unceasing prayer.[11]

St. Maximos the Confessor
II, *Second Century on Love*, sec. 61

12 Enmity is considered not only alien to the life of prayer, but as an enemy of prayer. Here Maximos exhorts us to accept an apology (if made), or to assume that we are at fault. The point is not to establish who is right, but to be forgiving and humble.

13 Maximos provides practical guidance for each part of the soul and body. The Eastern approach is holistic.

Has a brother been the occasion of some trial for you and has your resentment led you to hatred? Do not let yourself be overcome by this hatred, but conquer it with love. You will succeed in this by praying to God sincerely for your brother and by accepting his apology; or else by conciliating him with an apology yourself, by regarding yourself as responsible for the trial, and by patiently waiting until the cloud has passed.[12]

> ST. MAXIMOS THE CONFESSOR
> II, *FOURTH CENTURY ON LOVE*, SEC. 22

If you want to be a just person, assign to each aspect of yourself—to your soul and your body—what accords with it. To the intelligent aspect of the soul, assign spiritual reading, contemplation, and prayer; to the incensive aspect, spiritual love, the opposite of hatred; to the desiring aspect, moderation and self-control; to the fleshly part, food and clothing, for these alone are necessary (1 Timothy 6:8).[13]

> ST. MAXIMOS THE CONFESSOR
> II, *FOURTH CENTURY ON LOVE*, SEC. 44

Who in this generation is completely free from impassioned conceptual images, and has been granted uninterrupted, pure, and spiritual prayer? Yet this is the mark of the inner monk.

> ST. MAXIMOS THE CONFESSOR
> II, *FOURTH CENTURY ON LOVE*, SEC. 51

14 Maximos is one of numerous Fathers who writes about the importance of the Lord's Prayer as the model for the prayer of the Christian.

15 By "noetic eyes," Abba Philimon is referring to the "eyes" of the *nous,* the spiritual intellect by which we apprehend God.

Since, then, prayer is petition for the blessings given by the incarnate Logos, let us make him our teacher in prayer. And when we have contemplated the sense of each phrase as carefully as possible, let us confidently set it forth; for the Logos himself gives us, in the manner that is best for us, the capacity to understand what he says. "Our Father, who art in heaven, hallowed be thy name; thy kingdom come" (Matthew 6:9–10). It is appropriate that at the outset the Lord should teach those who pray to start with theology, and should initiate them into the mode of existence of him who is by essence the creative Cause of all things. For these opening words of the prayer contain a revelation of the Father, of the name of the Father, and of the kingdom of the Father, so that from this beginning we may be taught to revere, invoke, and worship the Trinity in unity.[14]

St. Maximos the Confessor
II, On the Lord's Prayer

Love and self-control purify the soul, while pure prayer illumines the intellect.

St. Thalassios the Libyan
II, On Love, Self-Control and Life in Accordance
with the Intellect, First Century, sec. 11

Just as love and self-control destroy evil thoughts, so contemplation and prayer destroy all exaltation.

St. Thalassios the Libyan
II, On Love, Self-Control and Life in Accordance
with the Intellect, Third Century, sec. 13

For through unceasing prayer and the study of the divine Scriptures the soul's noetic eyes are opened, and they see the King of the celestial powers, and great joy and fierce longing burn intensely in the soul; and as the flesh, too, is taken up by the Spirit, man becomes wholly spiritual.[15]

Abba Philimon
II, A Discourse on Abba Philimon

88

16 Ilias says here that bodily fasting is not simply useful for spiritual advancement, but is in fact necessary for prayer.

17 Ilias the Presbyter and Ekdikos (late eleventh to early twelfth century) was a lawyer and judge who was later ordained a priest. His writings suggest that he was influenced by the tradition of prayer at St. Catherine's Monastery on Mount Sinai, and they are a harbinger of spiritual theology associated with Gregory Palamas and the hesychasts.

Nothing is better than pure prayer. From it, as from a spring, come the virtues: understanding and gentleness, love and self-control, and the support and encouragement that God grants in response to tears. The beauty of pure prayer is made manifest when the mind dwells in the realm of intelligible realities alone and our longing to attain what is divine is endless.

ST. THEOGNOSTOS
II, ON THE PRACTICE OF THE VIRTUES, SEC. 5

Strength to pray lies in the deliberate privation of food, and strength to go without food lies in not seeing or hearing about worldly things except when strictly necessary. He who is negligent in this fails to build his fasting on a firm foundation, and so he brings about the collapse of the whole edifice of prayer, which itself is based on fasting.[16]

ILIAS THE PRESBYTER[17]
III, GNOMIC ANTHOLOGY I, SEC. 3

Spiritual work can exist even without bodily labor. Blessed, therefore, is the man who regards spiritual work as superior to physical work: through the first he makes up any deficiency where the second is concerned, because he lives the hidden life of prayer that is manifest to God.

ILIAS THE PRESBYTER
III, GNOMIC ANTHOLOGY I, SEC. 86

The uninitiated intellect is not permitted to enter the ripe vineyard of prayer. It is given access only—and barely—to the literal repetition of the psalms, as a poor man is allowed to glean the small grapes left on the vines.

ILIAS THE PRESBYTER
III, GNOMIC ANTHOLOGY IV, SEC. 63

18 Gratitude is an essential characteristic of the Christian. Indeed, the central act of Christian worship—the Eucharist—is the Greek word that means "thanksgiving."

19 Here imageless prayer is seen as necessary to defeat the devil's attempts to distract us from true prayer. Peter also reminds us that words are useless unless they are expressing the prayerful state of the *nous.*

The intellect that closes itself within the mind during prayer is like a bridegroom conversing with the bride inside the bridal chamber. But the intellect that is not allowed to enter stands dejectedly outside, crying: "Who will lead me into the walled city?" (Psalm 60:9). Who will guide me until I no longer see vanities and delusions during prayer?

ILIAS THE PRESBYTER
III, *GNOMIC ANTHOLOGY IV*, SEC. 67

Let him who wants to act rightly entreat God in prayer, and at once knowledge and power will be given to him. In this way it will be evident that the grace bestowed by God was justly given; for it was given after prayer, although it could have been given without prayer. No praise, however, is due to the man who accepts the air by means of which he lives, knowing that without it life is impossible; rather he himself owes thanks to his Creator, who has given him a nose and the health to breathe and live. Similarly, we also should rather thank God because in his grace he has created our prayer, our knowledge, our strength, our virtue, all our circumstances, and our very selves. And not only has he done all this, but he ceaselessly does whatever he can to overcome our wickedness and that of our enemies, the demons.[18]

ST. PETER OF DAMASKOS
III, *A TREASURY OF DIVINE KNOWLEDGE*, INTRODUCTION

The devil will fail in his purpose if we apply the counsel of the holy fathers: that during the time of prayer we should keep our intellect free from form, shape, and color, and not give access to anything at all, whether light, fire, or anything else; and that we should do all we can to confine our mind solely to the words we are saying, since he who prays only with his mouth prays to the wind and not to God. For, unlike men, God is attentive to the intellect and not to the words spoken.[19]

ST. PETER OF DAMASKOS
III, *A TREASURY OF DIVINE KNOWLEDGE*, INTRODUCTION

[20] Peter gives voice here to the Eastern understanding of prayer as physical, as well as spiritual. Orthodoxy sees the human being as psychosomatic—that is, as an embodied soul or an ensouled body. Thus, the physical affects the spiritual and the spiritual affects the physical. For this reason Orthodox worship is very physical, not only in effort (as with prostrations) but with all five senses. The church is filled with icons of Christ and the saints, lit candles, the smoke and smell of incense, and so on.

The fourth form of discipline consists in the recital of psalms—that is to say, in prayer expressed in a bodily way through psalms and prostrations. This is in order to gall the body and humble the soul, so that our enemies the demons may take flight and our allies the angels come to us, and we may know from where we receive help.[20] Otherwise, in ignorance we may grow arrogant, thinking that what we do is due to ourselves. If that happens, we will be forsaken by God so that we may recognize our own weakness. The fifth form of discipline consists of spiritual prayer, prayer that is offered by the intellect and free from all thoughts. During such prayer the intellect is concentrated within the words spoken and, inexpressibly contrite, it abases itself before God, asking only that His will may be done in all its pursuits and conceptions. It does not pay attention to any thought, shape, color, light, fire, or anything at all of this kind; but, conscious that it is watched by God and communing with him alone, it is free from form, color, and shape. Such is the pure prayer appropriate for those still engaged in ascetic practice; for the contemplative there are yet higher forms of prayer.

ST. PETER OF DAMASKOS
III, *A TREASURY OF DIVINE KNOWLEDGE*, INTRODUCTION

Each time a godlike thought comes to us spontaneously, suddenly, and without our knowing how, … we should always at once abandon every worldly concern and even our rule of prayer. We should do this in order to guard, as the apple of our eye, whatever spiritual knowledge or compunction it may bring, until, through God's providence, it withdraws from us.

ST. PETER OF DAMASKOS
III, *A TREASURY OF DIVINE KNOWLEDGE*, SPURIOUS KNOWLEDGE

21 While it seems strange to Protestant Christians in particular, Orthodox Christians pray for the departed, confident that such prayers may
aid in the salvation of those who have "fallen asleep." The East emphasizes the teaching of Jesus that "God is not God of the dead but of
the living" (Mark 12:27), meaning that those who have fallen asleep
are not dead to God. (Jesus was referring to Abraham, Isaac, and
Jacob.) "Fallen asleep" is a Christian term for death that is first mentioned by Paul in 1 Thessalonians 4:13. This phrase is not a euphemism
but instead reflects the Christian conviction that all are alive to God
in Christ.

22 Prayer is the very experience of God.

23 The language of rapture is not uncommon among Christian spiritual
writers. It is not surprising, for example, that spiritual writers are often
moved to write about the Song of Songs in the Hebrew Bible, in which
the relationship of God to the human being is understood in terms of
the marital image of sexual union.

24 True theology is not a human activity, as when we think and write
about God. It is the gift of God the Trinity's own self.

We then pray for the departed, that they may receive salvation so as to remind ourselves of our own death. It is a sign of love to pray for all men, even when we need the prayers of all. We also pray to be directed by God and to become what he wishes us to be; and to be united with others, so that through their prayers we may receive mercy, all the while regarding them as superior to ourselves.[21]

St. Peter of Damaskos

III, *A Treasury of Divine Knowledge*, Spurious Knowledge

For it is said of God that he "gives prayer to him who prays" (1 Samuel 2:9, LXX); and, indeed, to one who truly prays the prayer of the body, God gives the prayer of the intellect; and to one who diligently cultivates the prayer of the intellect, God gives the imageless and formless prayer that comes from the pure fear of him. Again, to one who practices this prayer effectively, God grants the contemplation of created beings. Once this is attained—once the intellect has freed itself from all things and, not content with hearing about God secondhand,[22] devotes itself to him in action and thought—God permits the intellect to be seized in rapture,[23] conferring on it the gift of true theology[24] and the blessings of the age to be.

St. Peter of Damaskos

III, *Conscious Awareness in the Heart*

25 Makarios makes it clear that our ascetic efforts in prayer are not actions designed to earn merit, but are simply our cooperation with God in protecting the grace of prayer that God gives to us.

26 Makarios reminds us that different gifts are needed and practiced in the Christian community, and those who practice one ministry have no basis for seeing themselves as greater than those who practice another ministry. The key to the practice of any ministry is "simplicity before others, guilelessness, mutual love, joy, and humility of every kind."

He who cultivates prayer has to fight with all diligence and watchfulness, all endurance, all struggle of soul and toil of body, so that he does not become sluggish and surrender himself to distraction of thought, to excessive sleep, to listlessness, debility, and confusion, or defile himself with turbulent and indecent suggestions, yielding his mind to things of this kind, satisfied merely with standing or kneeling for a long time, while his intellect wanders far away. For unless a person has been trained in strict vigilance, so that when attacked by a flood of useless thoughts he tests and sifts through them all, yearning always for the Lord, he is readily seduced in many unseen ways by the devil. Moreover, those not yet capable of persisting in prayer can easily grow arrogant, thus allowing the machinations of evil to destroy the good work in which they are engaged and making a present of it to the devil. Unless humility and love, simplicity and goodness regulate our prayer, this prayer—or, rather, this pretense of prayer—cannot profit us at all.[25]

ST. MAKARIOS OF EGYPT
III, *PRAYER*, SEC. 21–22

Simplicity before others, guilelessness, mutual love, joy, and humility of every kind, must be laid down as the foundation of the community. Otherwise, disparaging others or grumbling about them, we make our labor profitless. He who persists ceaselessly in prayer must not disparage the man incapable of doing this, nor must the man who devotes himself to serving the needs of the community complain about those who are dedicated to prayer. For if both the prayers and the service are offered in a spirit of simplicity and love for others, the superabundance of those dedicated to prayer will make up for the insufficiency of those who serve, and vice versa.[26] In this way the equality that St. Paul commends is maintained (2 Corinthians 8:14): he who has much does not have to excess and he who has little has no lack (Exodus 16:18).

ST. MAKARIOS OF EGYPT
III, *PRAYER*, SEC. 26

+ "Some there are who say that prayer beguiles. This is not so. A man is beguiled by listening to his own self, and not by prayer. All the saints lived in prayer, and called others to prayer. Prayer is the path to God. By prayer we obtain humility, patience and every good gift. The man who speaks against prayer has manifestly never experienced the goodness of the Lord, and how greatly He loves us. No evil ever comes from God. All the saints prayed without ceasing: they filled every moment with prayer."

—St. Silouan of Athos,
The Way of Christ: Gospel, Spiritual Life and Renewal in Orthodoxy

Prayer rightly combined with understanding is superior to every virtue
and commandment. The Lord himself testifies to this. For in the house
of Martha and Mary he contrasted Martha, who was engaged in
looking after him, with Mary, who sat at his feet joyfully drinking the
ambrosia of his divine words.... He said this not in order to disparage
acts of service, but so as to distinguish clearly what is higher from
what is lower.

ST. MAKARIOS OF EGYPT
III, *PRAYER*, SEC. 32

You should look on all who are in the monastery as saints and regard
only yourself as a sinner and as least of all, thinking that on that day
all will be saved and you alone will be punished. And when you are in
church reflecting about these things, weep bitter tears of
compunction, taking no account of those who will be shocked by this
or mock such behavior. But if you see that as a result of this you are
slipping into self-esteem, leave the church and weep in secret,
returning as soon as you can to your place. This is particularly valuable
in the case of beginners, especially during the six psalms, the psalter,
the readings, and the Divine Liturgy. Be careful not to condemn
anyone, but keep it in mind that all who see your distress will think
that you are a great sinner and will pray for your salvation. If you think
of this at all times and carry it out constantly, you will be greatly
helped, attracting to yourself God's grace and becoming a participant
in his divine blessings.

ST. SYMEON THE NEW THEOLOGIAN
IV, *PRACTICAL AND THEOLOGICAL TEXTS*, SEC. 123

27 Unceasing prayer is an inner activity of the intellect, and the lack of outward expression does not mean that it has ceased.

28 The other person always takes precedence over prayer. As Jesus said, "Truly I tell you, just as you did it to the least of these who are members of my family, you did it to me" (Matthew 25:40).

29 Although it is helpful to plan the time and place of prayer, Nikitas reminds us that we must not limit our prayer to the time and place we have set aside for prayer. Prayer may occupy us anywhere and anytime.

Unceasing prayer is prayer that does not leave the soul day or night. In consists not in what is outwardly perceived—outstretched hands, bodily stance, or verbal utterance—but in our inner concentration on the intellect's activity and on mindfulness of God born of unwavering compunction; and it can be perceived noetically by those capable of such perception.[27]

NIKITAS STITHATOS
IV, ON THE INNER NATURE OF THINGS AND
ON THE PURIFICATION OF THE INTELLECT, SEC. 74

If while you are singing a song of prayer to God, and one of your brethren knocks at the door of your cell, do not opt for the work of prayer rather than that of love and ignore your brother, for to act in that way would be alien to God. God desires love's mercy, not the sacrifice of prayer (Hosea 6:6). Rather, put aside the gift of prayer and speak with healing love to your brother. Then with tears and a contrite heart once more offer your gift of prayer to the Father of the spiritual powers, and a righteous spirit will be renewed within you (Matthew 5:23–24; Psalm 51:10, 17).[28]

NIKITAS STITHATOS
IV, ON THE INNER NATURE OF THINGS AND
ON THE PURIFICATION OF THE INTELLECT, SEC. 76

The mystery of prayer is not consummated at a certain specific time or place. For if you restrict prayer to particular times or places, you will waste the rest of the time in vain pursuits. Prayer may be defined as the intellect's unceasing intercourse with God. Its task is to engage the soul totally in things divine, its fulfillment—to adapt the words of St. Paul (1 Corinthians 6:17)—lies in so wedding the mind to God that it becomes one spirit with him.[29]

NIKITAS STITHATOS
IV, ON THE INNER NATURE OF THINGS AND
ON THE PURIFICATION OF THE INTELLECT, SEC. 77

+ "The basic presupposition for the practice of inner prayer is therefore
the conviction that this is not a simple prayer, but rather that it is communion and union with God. The inaccessible God is present and
makes himself attainable for us through his divine energies. God
descends on us through the prayer and unites himself with us, with us
sinners. And, because we take Christ into ourselves, we clearly obtain
with him the Father through the Holy Spirit. The Word who became
flesh in history in Palestine, the Word of God who carries all creation on
his fingertip, now allows himself to be grasped by us when we say the
Jesus Prayer. Christ enters into us, dwells with us, walks with us."

—Archimandrite Aemilianos,
*The Living Witness of the Holy Mountain: Contemporary Voices from
Mount Athos*

If you are seated and you see that prayer is continuously active in your heart, do not abandon it and get up to psalmodize until in God's good time it leaves you of its own accord. Otherwise, abandoning the interior presence of God, you will address yourself to him from without, thus passing from a higher to a lower state, provoking unrest, and disrupting the intellect's serenity.

ST. GREGORY OF SINAI
IV, ON PRAYER, SEC. 5

1 The writers of the *Philokalia* are practitioners of hesychastic prayer—
that is, the prayer is one of "stillness" (*hesychia* in Greek).

2 Both the Lord Jesus and the Holy Spirit are present in prayer in that,
as Irenaeus of Lyons (ca. 130–202) tells us, they are the "two hands
of the Father" in the world.

4 □ The Jesus Prayer

Attentiveness is the heart's stillness, unbroken by any thought.[1] In this stillness the heart breathes and invokes, endlessly and without ceasing, only Jesus Christ who is the Son of God and himself God. It confesses him who alone has power to forgive our sins, and with his aid it courageously faces its enemies. Through this invocation enfolded continually in Christ, who secretly divines all hearts, the soul does everything it can to keep its sweetness and its inner struggle hidden from men, so that the devil, coming upon it surreptitiously, does not lead it into evil and destroy its precious work.

St. Hesychios the Priest
I, *On Watchfulness and Holiness*, sec. 5

In the presence of Christ you will feel the Holy Spirit spring up within your soul. It is the Spirit who initiates man's intellect, so that it can see with "unveiled face" (2 Corinthians 3:18). For "No one can say 'Lord Jesus' except in the Holy Spirit" (1 Corinthians 12:3). In other words, it is the Spirit who mystically confirms Christ's presence in us.[2]

St. Hesychios the Priest
I, *On Watchfulness and Holiness*, sec. 29

+ "If you see, Gregory [of Sinai] says, the impurity of evil spirits in the thoughts that are presented in your mind, do not be frightened and do not wonder, even if such thoughts seem good to you. Do not give any attention to them, but control your breathing as much as you can and enclose your mind in your heart, as you arm yourself by calling on the Lord Jesus. Appeal to him, as often and consciously as possible, and the thoughts will dissolve as they are burnt up by the fiery, invisible rays radiating from your calling on the divine Name."

—St. Nil Sorsky,
Nil Sorsky: The Complete Writings

3 The Jesus Prayer is an effective means of dealing with distraction and supporting watchfulness.

Those who lack experience should know that it is only through the unceasing watchfulness of our intellect and the constant invocation of Jesus Christ, our Creator and God, that we, coarse and cloddish in mind and body as we are, can overcome our bodiless and invisible enemies; for not only are they subtle, swift, malevolent, and skilled in malice, but they have an experience in warfare gained over all the years since Adam. The inexperienced have as weapons the Jesus Prayer and the impulse to discern what is from God. The experienced have the best method and teacher of all: the activity, discernment, and peace of God himself.

ST. HESYCHIOS THE PRIEST
I, *ON WATCHFULNESS AND HOLINESS*, SEC. 42

Watchfulness and the Jesus Prayer, as I have said, mutually reinforce one another; for close attentiveness goes with constant prayer, while prayer goes with close watchfulness and attentiveness of intellect.

ST. HESYCHIOS THE PRIEST
I, *ON WATCHFULNESS AND HOLINESS*, SEC. 94

Whenever we are filled with evil thoughts, we should throw the invocation of our Lord Jesus Christ into their midst. Then, as experience has taught us, we shall see them instantly dispersed like smoke in the air. Once the intellect is left to itself again, we can renew our constant attentiveness and our invocation. Whenever we are distracted, we should act in this way.[3]

ST. HESYCHIOS THE PRIEST
I, *ON WATCHFULNESS AND HOLINESS*, SEC. 98

Forgetfulness can extinguish our guard over our intellect as water extinguishes fire; but the continuous repetition of the Jesus Prayer, combined with strict watchfulness, uproots it from our heart. The Jesus Prayer requires watchfulness as a lantern requires a candle.

ST. HESYCHIOS THE PRIEST
I, *ON WATCHFULNESS AND HOLINESS*, SEC. 102

4 By "single-phrased Jesus Prayer" is meant the prayer "Lord Jesus Christ, Son of God, have mercy on me."

We will travel the road of repentance correctly if, as we begin to give attention to the intellect, we combine humility with watchfulness, and prayer with the power to rebut evil thoughts. In this way we will adorn the chamber of our heart with the holy and venerable name of Jesus Christ as with a lighted lamp, and we will sweep our heart clean of wickedness, purifying and embellishing it.

ST. HESYCHIOS THE PRIEST
I, ON WATCHFULNESS AND HOLINESS, SEC. 152

The single-phrased Jesus Prayer destroys and consumes the deceits of the demons.[4] For when we invoke Jesus, God and Son of God, constantly and tirelessly, he does not allow them to project in the mind's mirror even the first hint of their infiltration—that is to say, their provocation—or any form, nor does he allow them to have any converse with the heart.

ST. HESYCHIOS THE PRIEST
I, ON WATCHFULNESS AND HOLINESS, SEC. 174

A ship does not go far without water; and there is no progress whatsoever in the guarding of the intellect without watchfulness, humility, and the Jesus Prayer. Stones form the foundation of a house; but the foundation of sanctity—and its roof—is the holy and venerable name of our Lord Jesus Christ.... We write of what we know; and for those who want to understand what we say, we bear witness to all that we have seen as we journeyed on our path.... The sun cannot shine without light; nor can the heart be cleansed of the stain of destructive thoughts without invoking in prayer the name of Jesus. This being the case, we should use that name as we do our own breath. For that name is light, while evil thoughts are darkness; it is God and Master, while evil thoughts are slaves and demons.

ST. HESYCHIOS THE PRIEST
I, ON WATCHFULNESS AND HOLINESS, SEC. 168–170

5 | The Jesus Prayer is useful for ridding the intellect of evil thoughts. Rather than focusing on the evil thoughts and feeling guilt over their occurrence, we ought to simply say the Jesus Prayer, confident that it will rid us of these malicious thoughts.

6 | The practice of the Jesus Prayer in Orthodox tradition was revived in the twentieth-century Christian practice of Centering Prayer, a movement also known as contemplative prayer.

Noxious foods give trouble when taken into the body; but as soon as he feels the pain, the person who has eaten them can quickly take some emetic and so be unharmed. Similarly, once the intellect that has imbibed evil thoughts senses their bitterness, it can easily expel them and get rid of them completely by means of the Jesus Prayer, uttered from the depths of the heart. This lesson, and the experience corresponding to it, have by God's grace conveyed understanding to those who practice watchfulness.[5]

ST. HESYCHIOS THE PRIEST
I, ON WATCHFULNESS AND HOLINESS, SEC. 188

Truly blessed is the man whose mind and heart are as closely attached to the Jesus Prayer and to the ceaseless invocation of his name as air to the body or flames to the wax.[6] The sun rising over the earth creates the daylight; and the venerable and holy name of the Lord Jesus, shining continually in the mind, gives birth to countless intellections as radiant as the sun.

ST. HESYCHIOS THE PRIEST
I, ON WATCHFULNESS AND HOLINESS, SEC. 196

He who has attained perfect love, and has ordered his whole life in accordance with it, is the person who says "Lord Jesus" in the Holy Spirit (1 Corinthians 12:3).

ST. MAXIMOS THE CONFESSOR
II, FOURTH CENTURY ON LOVE, SEC. 39

7 | Like the Jesus Prayer, Psalms may be prayed as a means of keeping watch over the intellect. But no matter which is used, it is important that our thoughts be focused on the words and not elsewhere.

8 | When Philotheos speaks of slaughtering "all the sinners in the land," he is not referring to people but to evil thoughts.

9 | Jesus alone, and not our efforts, saves. Salvation is always a gift from God, and can never be earned by our works.

Pay strict attention to your heart and watch over it, so that it does not give admittance to your thoughts that are evil or in any way vain and useless. Without interruption, whether asleep or awake, eating, drinking, or in company, let your heart inwardly and mentally at times be meditating on the Psalms, at other times be repeating the prayer, "Lord Jesus Christ, Son of God, have mercy on me." And when you chant, make sure that your mouth is not saying one thing while your mind is thinking about another.[7]

ABBA PHILIMON
II, *A DISCOURSE ON ABBA PHILIMON*, SEC. 11

When engaged in noetic warfare, we should therefore do all we can to choose some spiritual practice from divine Scripture and apply it to our intellect like a healing ointment. From dawn we should stand bravely and unflinchingly at the gate of the heart, with true remembrance of God and unceasing prayer of Jesus Christ in the soul; and keeping watch with the intellect, we should slaughter all the sinners in the land (Psalm 101:8, LXX).[8]

ST. PHILOTHEOS OF SINAI
III, *FORTY TEXTS ON WATCHFULNESS*, SEC. 2

The blessed remembrance of God—which is the very presence of Jesus—with a heart full of wrath and a saving animosity against the demons, dissolves all trickeries of thought, plots, argumentation, fantasies, obscure conjectures, and, in short, everything with which the destroyer arms himself and that he insolently deploys in his attempt to swallow our souls. When Jesus is invoked, he promptly burns up everything. For our salvation lies in Christ Jesus alone. The Savior himself made this clear when he said: "Without me you can do nothing" (John 15:5).[9]

ST. PHILOTHEOS OF SINAI
III, *FORTY TEXTS ON WATCHFULNESS*, SEC. 22

[+] "The prayer of Jesus is not an occasional petition that we direct to God. It is in fact our own deification. There would be no reason to stay all day in conversation with God if it were simply a matter of addressing words to him. God hears very well, even to the noises of our bowels. There would be no need to pray day and night. Rather, the prayer consists before all in feeding upon Christ, the Lamb of God, and of drinking the Savior himself, by the invocation of his holy name. It is an intoxicating beverage, one that carries man into the heavens. It is the whole Christ whom we then absorb, and we become thus participants in God, reflecting—as Christ himself—the divine attributes."

—Archimandrite Aemilianos,
The Living Witness of the Holy Mountain:
Contemporary Voices from Mount Athos

[10] Ilias is using an image from the Jewish Temple in Jerusalem.

Smoke from wood kindling a fire troubles the eyes; but then the fire gives them light and gladdens them. Similarly, unceasing attentiveness is irksome; but when, invoked in prayer, Jesus draws near, he illumines the heart; for remembrance of him confers on us spiritual enlightenment and the highest of all blessings.

ST. PHILOTHEOS OF SINAI
III, *FORTY TEXTS ON WATCHFULNESS*, SEC. 29

Evidence of an intellect devoted to God is its absorption in the single-phrased Jesus Prayer; of an adroit intelligence, opportune speech; of a nonattached sense-perception, simplicity in taste. When such evidence is present in all three cases, the soul's powers are said to be in good health.

ILIAS THE PRESBYTER
III, *A GNOMIC ANTHOLOGY*, PART II, SEC. 94

He who is distracted during prayer stands outside the first veil. He who undistractedly offers the single-phrased Jesus Prayer is within the veil. But he alone has glimpsed the Holy of Holies who, with his natural thoughts at rest, contemplates that which transcends every intellect, and who has in this way been granted to some extent a vision of the divine light.[10]

ILIAS THE PRESBYTER
III, *A GNOMIC ANTHOLOGY*, PART II, SEC. 104

Apt silence bridles anger; moderation in food bridles mindless desire; and the single-phrased Jesus Prayer bridles unruly thought.... The spiritual aspirant must restrain his sense through frugality and his intellect through the single-phrased Jesus Prayer. Having in this way detached himself from the passions, he will find himself caught up to the Lord during prayer.

ILIAS THE PRESBYTER
III, *A GNOMIC ANTHOLOGY*, PART IV, SEC. 65, 75

11 There is freedom in the method each person chooses for saying the Jesus Prayer. Gregory simply advises that we should not change methods often; consistency in practice is important to spiritual growth. When it comes to the question of whether to pray it aloud or silently with the intellect, Gregory advises the use of both. We see this same flexibility in the modern resurgence of contemplation known as Centering Prayer.

Some of the fathers advise us to say the whole prayer, "Lord Jesus Christ, Son of God, have mercy," while others specify that we say it in two parts—"Lord Jesus Christ, have mercy," and then "Son of God, help me"—because this is easier, given the immaturity and feebleness of our intellect. For no one on his own account and without the help of the Spirit can mystically invoke the Lord Jesus, for this can be done with purity and in its fullness only with the help of the Holy Spirit (1 Corinthians 12:3). Like children who can still speak only falteringly, we are unable by ourselves to articulate the prayer properly. Yet we must not out of laziness frequently change the words of the invocation, but only do this rarely, so as to ensure continuity. Again, some fathers teach that the prayer should be said aloud; others that it should be said silently with the intellect. On the basis of my personal experience, I recommend both ways. For at times the intellect grows listless and cannot repeat the prayer, while at other times the same thing happens to the voice. Thus we should pray both vocally and in the intellect. But when we pray vocally we should speak quietly and calmly and not loudly, so that the voice does not disturb and hinder the intellect's consciousness and concentration. This is always a danger until the intellect grows accustomed to its work, makes progress, and receives power from the Spirit to pray firmly and with complete attention. Then there will be no need to pray aloud—indeed, it will be impossible, for we shall be content to carry out the whole work with the intellect alone.[11]

ST. GREGORY OF SINAI
IV, ON PRAYER, SEC. 2

12 Gregory emphasizes here that the Jesus Prayer is to be imageless. He also counsels against timidity in prayer. As Paul writes, "For all who are led by the spirit of God are sons of God. For you did not receive the spirit of slavery to fall back into fear, but you have received the spirit of sonship. When we cry, 'Abba! Father!' it is the Spirit himself bearing witness with our spirit that we are children of God" (Romans 8:14–16).

Authentic prayer—the warmth that accompanies the Jesus Prayer, for
it is Jesus who enkindles fire on the earth of our hearts (Luke 12:49)—
consumes the passions like thorns and fills the soul with delight and
joyfulness. Such prayer comes neither from right nor left, nor from
above, but wells up in the heart like a spring of water from the life-
quickening Spirit. It is this prayer alone that you should aspire to
realize and possess in your heart, always keeping your intellect free
from images, concepts, and thoughts. And do not be afraid, for he
who says, "Take heart; it is I; be not afraid" (Matthew 14:27), is with
us—he whom we seek and who protects us always. When we invoke
God we must be neither timid nor hesitant.[12]

ST. GREGORY OF SINAI
IV, *ON PRAYER*, SEC. 7

The intellectual activity consisting of thought and intuition is called
intellect, and the power that activates thought and intuition is likewise
the intellect; and this power Scripture also calls the *heart*. It is because
the intellect is preeminent among our inner powers that our soul is
deiform [Godlike]. In those devoted to prayer, and especially to the
single-phrased Jesus Prayer, the intellect's noetic activity is easily
ordered and purified; but the power that produces this activity cannot
be purified unless all the soul's other powers are also purified. Thus, if
one of its powers is vitiated, the whole of it is defiled; for since the soul
is single, the evil in one of its powers is communicated to all the rest.

ST. GREGORY PALAMAS
IV, *THREE TEXTS ON PRAYER AND PURITY OF HEART*, SEC. 2

13 Theoliptos, Metropolitan of Philadelphia (ca. 1250–1332), was a monk who later served as the metropolitan (the ruling bishop) of Philadelphia. His teaching was very influential on one of his young disciples, Gregory Palamas.

14 As indicated earlier, baptism is not magic. To be effective, it requires both obedience to the commandments of God and the continuous repetition of the Jesus Prayer under the guidance of a spiritual father or mother.

Do not neglect prostration. It provides an image of man's fall into sin and expresses the confession of our sinfulness. Getting up, on the other hand, signifies repentance and the promise to lead a life of virtue. Let each prostration be accompanied by a noetic invocation of Christ, so that by falling before the Lord in soul and body you may gain the grace of the God of souls and bodies.

THEOLIPTOS, METROPOLITAN OF PHILADELPHIA[13]
IV, ON INNER WORK IN CHRIST AND THE MONASTIC PROFESSION

Moreover, when your intellect is firmly established in your heart, it must not remain there silent and idle; it should constantly repeat and meditate upon the prayer, "Lord Jesus Christ, Son of God, have mercy on me," and should never stop doing this. For this prayer protects the intellect from distraction, renders it impregnable to diabolic attacks, and every day increases its love and desire for God.

NIKIPHOROS THE MONK
IV, ON WATCHFULNESS AND THE GUARDING OF THE HEART

The energy of the Holy Spirit, which we have already mystically received in baptism, is realized in two ways. First—to generalize—this gift is revealed, as St. Mark [the Ascetic] tells us, through arduous and protracted practice of the commandments: to the degree to which we effectively practice the commandments, its radiance is increasingly manifested in us. Second, it is manifested to those under spiritual guidance through the continuous invocation of the Lord Jesus, repeated with conscious awareness, that is, through mindfulness of God. In the first way, it is revealed more slowly, in the second more rapidly, if one diligently and persistently learns how to dig the ground and locate the gold.[14]

ST. GREGORY OF SINAI
IV, ON THE SIGNS OF GRACE AND DELUSION, SEC. 3

15 The cell is the room where the monk sleeps and prays. *Cell* comes from the Latin *coelum,* meaning "heaven." The monk, through prayer, can encounter heaven in his room.

There are two modes of union or, rather, two ways of entering into the noetic prayer that the Spirit activates in the heart. For either the intellect, cleaving to the Lord (1 Corinthians 6:17), is present in the heart prior to the action of the prayer; or the prayer itself, progressively quickened in the fire of spiritual joy, draws the intellect along with it or welds it to the invocation of the Lord Jesus and to union with him. For since the Spirit works in each person as he wishes (1 Corinthians 12:11), one of these two ways we have mentioned will take precedence in some people, the other in others. Sometimes, as the passions subside through the ceaseless invocation of Jesus Christ, a divine energy wells up in the heart, and a divine warmth is kindled; for Scripture says that our God is a fire that consumes the passions (Deuteronomy 4:24; Hebrews 12:29). At other times the Spirit draws the intellect to himself, confining it to the depths of the heart and restraining it from its usual distractions.

ST. GREGORY OF SINAI
IV, ON STILLNESS: FIFTEEN TEXTS, SEC. 1

From then on, from whatever side a distractive thought may appear, before it has come to completion and assumed a form, the intellect immediately drives it away and destroys it with the invocation of Jesus Christ. From this point onward the intellect begins to be full of rancor against the demons and, rousing its natural anger against its noetic enemies, it pursues them and strikes them down. The rest you will learn for yourself, with God's help, by keeping guard over your intellect and by retaining Jesus in your heart. As the saying goes, "Sit in your cell and it will teach you everything."[15]

ST. SYMEON THE NEW THEOLOGIAN
IV, THE THREE METHODS OF PRAYER

16 Here Symeon gives a specific manner for saying the Jesus Prayer that includes lowering the head and staring at the navel—a method also used in non-Christian religions of the East—which led some critics to dismiss the posture as "navel-gazing."

In the case of a beginner in the art of spiritual warfare, God alone can expel thoughts, for it is only those strong in such warfare who are in a position to wrestle with them and banish them. Yet even they do not achieve this by themselves, but they fight against them with God's assistance, clothed in the armor of his grace. So when thoughts invade you, in place of weapons call on the Lord Jesus frequently and persistently and they will retreat; for they cannot bear the warmth produced in the heart by prayer and they flee as if scorched by fire.

St. Gregory of Sinai
IV, On Prayer, sec. 4

Then sit down in a quiet cell, in a corner by yourself, and do what I tell you. Close the door, and withdraw your intellect from everything worthless and transient. Rest your beard on your chest, and focus your physical gaze, together with the whole of your intellect, on the center of your belly or navel. Restrain the drawing-in of breath through your nostrils, so as not to breathe easily, and search inside yourself with your intellect so as to find the place of the heart, where all the powers of the soul reside. To start with, you will find there darkness and an impenetrable density. Later, when you practice this task day and night, you will find, as though miraculously, an unceasing joy. For as soon as the intellect attains the place of the heart, at once it sees things of which it previously knew nothing. It sees the open space within the heart and it beholds itself entirely luminous and full of discrimination.[16]

St. Symeon the New Theologian
IV, The Three Methods of Prayer

1 Whereas some theologians in the West see our nature as totally depraved, Isaiah assumes here that our true nature is that given to us by God. Thus, our spiritual struggle is against what is unnatural—that is, sin.

2 Evagrios teaches that three demons are the gateway for the rest—gluttony, avarice, and that which moves us to seek the favor of others. We cannot be successful in the spiritual life unless we first defeat these three unnatural appetites.

5 □ The Passions

When the intellect grows strong, it makes ready to pursue the love that quenches all bodily passions and that prevents anything contrary to nature from gaining control over the heart. Then the intellect, struggling against what is contrary to nature, separates this from what is in accordance with nature.[1]

ST. ISAIAH THE SOLITARY
I, ON GUARDING THE INTELLECT, SEC. 19

Of the demons opposing us in the practice of the ascetic life, there are three groups who fight in the front line: those who are entrusted with the appetites of gluttony, those who suggest avaricious thoughts, and those who incite us to seek the esteem of men. All the other demons follow behind and in their turn attack those already wounded by the first three groups.... That is why the devil suggested these three thoughts to the Savior: first he exhorted him to turn stones into bread; then he promised him the whole world, if Christ would fall down and worship him; and third he said that, if our Lord would listen to him, he would be glorified and suffer nothing in falling from the pinnacle of the Temple. But our Lord, having shown himself superior to these temptations, commanded the devil to "get behind him." In this way he teaches us that it is not possible to drive away the devil, unless we scornfully reject these three thoughts.[2]

EVAGRIOS THE SOLITARY
I, TEXTS ON DISCRIMINATION IN RESPECT OF
PASSIONS AND THOUGHTS, SEC. 1

3 Here Evagrios offers one of the reasons to avoid images in prayer—if we wish to see God who is without form or concept, we should avoid forms or concepts as things that might lead us away from God.

4 Peace is primarily an inner state and not an outer absence of violence.

5 Orthodox Christians avoid using the term *original sin* because it typically includes concepts alien to their theological tradition. In the West, it has been taught that all humans have inherited the guilt of Adam's sin in the Garden of Eden. This theology began with Jerome's (331–420) mistranslation of Romans 5:12. Paul said in that verse that since all sin, all die. But Jerome translated it as saying that in Adam "all have sinned." Because Augustine of Hippo (354–430) could not read Greek, he relied on Jerome's mistranslation and created a theology of original sin and original guilt to match the mistranslation. Modern translations—Roman Catholic and Protestant—have corrected Jerome's error.

What state, then, does the intellect need so that it can reach out to its Lord without deflection and commune with him without intermediary? When Moses tried to draw near to the burning bush, he was forbidden to approach until he had removed the sandals from his feet (Exodus 3:5). If, then, you wish to behold and commune with him who is beyond sense-perception and beyond concept, you must free yourself from every impassioned thought.[3]

EVAGRIOS THE SOLITARY
I, *ON PRAYER*, SEC. 3–4

Pray first for the purification of the passions; second, for deliverance from ignorance and forgetfulness; and third, for deliverance from all temptation, trial, and dereliction.

EVAGRIOS THE SOLITARY
I, *ON PRAYER*, SEC. 38

Peace is deliverance from the passions, and is not found except through the action of the Holy Spirit.[4]

ST. MARK THE ASCETIC
I, *ON THE SPIRITUAL LAW*, SEC. 192

A passion that we allow to grow active within us through our own choice afterwards forces itself upon us against our will.

ST. MARK THE ASCETIC
I, *ON THOSE WHO THINK THEY ARE MADE RIGHTEOUS BY WORKS*, SEC. 85

He who hates the passions gets rid of their causes. But he who is attracted by their causes is attacked by the passions, even though he does not wish it. When evil thoughts become active within us, we should blame ourselves and not ancestral sin.[5]

ST. MARK THE ASCETIC
I, *ON THOSE WHO THINK THEY ARE MADE RIGHTEOUS BY WORKS*, SEC. 119–120

6 | Mark identifies a different list of primary demons than Evagrios did—ignorance, forgetfulness, and laziness. He believes that these are the doorways for the other demons that seek to keep us from God.

7 | Three aspects or powers of the soul are the intelligent, the incensive, and the appetitive (or desiring). These aspects of the soul are neutral; that is, they may be used in accordance with God's will or contrary to God's will.

Imagine that there are three powerful and mighty giants of the
Philistines.... When these three have been overthrown and slain, all
the power of the demons is fatally weakened. These three giants are
the vices already mentioned: ignorance, the source of all evils;ted:
forgetfulness, its close relation and helper; and laziness, which weaves
the dark shroud enveloping the soul in murk. This third vice supports
and strengthens the other two, consolidating them so that evil
becomes deep-rooted and persistent in the negligent soul. Laziness,
forgetfulness, and ignorance in their turn support and strengthen the
other passions. Helping one another, and unable to hold their
positions apart from one another, they are the mainstay and the chief
leaders of the devil's army. Through them the whole of this army
infiltrates the soul and is enabled to achieve its objectives, which
otherwise it could not do.[6]

ST. MARK THE ASCETIC
I, *LETTER TO NICOLAS THE SOLITARY*

Our desire should be directed toward God and toward holiness. Our
intelligence should control our incensive power and our desire with
wisdom and skill, regulating them, admonishing them, correcting
them, and ruling them as a king rules over his subjects. Then, even if
they rebel against it, our innermost intelligence will direct the passions
in a way that accords with God's will, for we shall have set it in charge
of them. The brother of the Lord declares: "He who does not lapse in
his inmost intelligence is a perfect man, able also to bridle the whole
body" (James 3:2). For the truth is that every sin and transgression is
brought about through these three aspects of the soul, just as every
virtue and good action is also produced through them.[7]

ST. HESYCHIOS THE PRIEST
I, *ON WATCHFULNESS AND HOLINESS*, SEC. 126

[+] "Love is what banishes from man's soul the cause of all passions, which according to the holy Fathers is selfishness. All evil within us, emanates from vanity which is the diseased love for one's own self. Hence, Our Church has ascetic endeavours. Without ascetic endeavours, there is no spiritual life, no struggle, no advancement. We obey, fast, keep vigils, labour with prostrations and stand on our feet for hours in order to be cleansed from our passions. If the Orthodox Church ceases to be ascetic, it ceases to be Orthodox. It no longer helps man to be rid of his passions and become a god by Grace."

—Archimandrite George, *The Deification as the Purpose of Man's Life*

[8] We are counseled to avoid adding new images to our minds, so that we may concentrate on eliminating the ones we already have stored in our memory.

The intellect, being good-natured and innocent, readily goes in pursuit of lawless fantasies; and it can be restrained only on condition that its intelligence, the ruler of the passions, always bridles it and holds it back.

St. Hesychios the Priest
I, On Watchfulness and Holiness, sec. 145

When we not only refrain from worldly actions but no longer call them to mind, we have attained true tranquility. This gives the soul the opportunity to look at the impressions previously stamped on the mind, and to struggle against each one and eliminate it. As long as we go on receiving new impressions, our intelligence is occupied with them and so it is not possible to erase the earlier ones. In consequence, our struggle to eradicate the passions is inevitably far harder, since these passions have become strong through being allowed to increase gradually; and now, like a river in full flood, they drown the soul's discernment with one fantasy after another.[8]

St. Neilos the Ascetic
I, Ascetic Discourse

9 The Fathers of the *Philokalia* repeatedly exhort us to destroy the passions when they are small like an ant and can be dealt with more easily than when we have allowed them to grow strong like a lion. The passions, temptations, and sins are always easiest to deal with when we nip them in the bud.

10 Sinful fantasies stored in our memory must be eradicated; otherwise, they will continue to surface and might cause a "relapse into ... wickedness."

The Psalms praise those who do not wait for the passions to grow to full strength but kill them in infancy: "Blessed is he who seizes your little ones and dashes them against the rock" (Psalm 137:9). Perhaps Job, too, is hinting at some such thing when, reflecting on the course of his life, he says that the rush and the flag flourish in the river, but wither when deprived of water (Job 8:11). And his statement that the "ant-lion" has perished for lack of food (Job 4:11, LXX) would seem to have a similar significance. Wishing to show how the passions ensnare us, he coined this composite name from the boldest of all creatures, the lion, and the most trivial, the ant. For the provocations of the passions begin with trivial fantasies, creeping up unnoticed like an ant; but eventually the passions grow to an enormous size and their attack is as dangerous as a lion's. One who is pursuing the spiritual way should therefore fight the passions when they approach like ants, hoping to deceive him by their trivial appearance. For if they are allowed to gain a lion's strength, it is hard to resist them and to refuse them the food they demand.[9]

ST. NEILOS THE ASCETIC
I, *ASCETIC DISCOURSE*

For if someone does not watch his mind attentively, he will find that, after he has cut down the passions, the images of past fantasies begin to emerge again like young shoots. If he constantly allows these images to force their way into his intellect and does not bar their entry, the passions will once more establish themselves within him; despite his previous victory, he will have to struggle against them again. For, after being tamed and taught to graze like cattle, the passions can become savage once more through our negligence and regain the ferocity of wild beasts. It is to prevent this that Scripture says, "Do not try to follow them after they have been destroyed before you" (Deuteronomy 12:30); that is, we must not allow our soul to form the habit of taking pleasure in fantasies of this kind, and so relapse into its previous wickedness.[10]

ST. NEILOS THE ASCETIC
I, *ASCETIC DISCOURSE*

11 Antony (251–356) was an ascetic in Egypt who is known as the "father of monasticism." His biography was written by Athanasios of Alexandria (ca. 296–373), who referred to him as the "physician of all Egypt." Antony is the prototype of the monastic elder or "old man" (*geronta* in Greek and *staretz* in Russian). The work that appears in the *Philokalia* under his name, *On the Character of Men and on the Virtuous Life*, is actually of non-Christian origin, reflecting platonic and stoic philosophy.

12 Our senses, like the aspects of the soul, are neutral. They may be used in accordance with God's will, or they can be exploited by distorted passions. Antony identifies four such passions—self-esteem, levity, anger, and cowardice.

If we try to cure bodily passions in order to avoid the ridicule of people we chance to meet, how much more should we try to cure the passions of the soul; for, when we are judged face to face by God, we shall not wish to be found worthless and ridiculous. Since we have free will, although we may desire to perform evil actions, we can avoid doing so; and it is in our power to live in accordance with God's will. Moreover, no one can ever force us to do what is evil against our will. It is through this struggle against evil that we shall become worthy to serve God and live like angels in heaven.

ST. ANTONY THE GREAT[11]
I, ON THE CHARACTER OF MEN, AND ON THE VIRTUOUS LIFE, SEC. 66

A soul engaged in spiritual training, being deiform, must now cower with fear in the face of the passions.... Man is attacked by his senses through the soul's passions. The bodily senses are five: sight, smell, hearing, taste, and touch. Through these five senses the unhappy soul is taken captive when it succumbs to its four passions. These four passions are self-esteem, levity, anger, and cowardice. When, therefore, a man through sound judgment and reflection has shown good generalship, he controls and defeats the passions. Then he is no longer attacked but his soul is at peace; and he is crowned by God, because he has conquered.[12]

ST. ANTONY THE GREAT
I, ON THE CHARACTER OF MEN, AND ON THE VIRTUOUS LIFE, SEC. 79

13 Because we cannot control what passions attack us, we are not morally responsible for the occurrence of such attacks. When we indulge the passions, when we allow them to "linger," then we do become morally culpable.

14 Theodoros provides a different list of the principal negative passions. He emphasizes that if we successfully battle the three chief ones (the love of sensual pleasure, riches, and praise), then we will, at the same time, defeat the lesser passions.

15 The Eastern tradition consistently interprets "dashing the children of Babylon against the stones" as referring to sins, not actual children. More specifically, it is taken as referring to the beginnings of sin—the first thought of sin before we assent to it and then commit it.

It does not lie within our power to decide whether or not the passions
are going to harass and attack the soul. But it does lie within our
power to prevent impassioned thoughts from lingering within us and
arousing the passions to action. The first of these conditions is not
sinful, inasmuch as it is outside our control; where the second is
concerned, if we fight against the passions and overcome them we are
rewarded, but we shall be punished if because of laziness and
cowardice we let them overcome us.[13]

ST. THEODOROS THE GREAT ASCETIC
II, *A CENTURY OF SPIRITUAL TEXTS*, SEC. 9

There are three principal passions, through which all the rest arise:
love of sensual pleasure, love of riches, and love of praise. Close in
their wake follow five other evil spirits, and from these five arise a
great swarm of passions and all manner of evil. Thus he who defeats
the three leaders and rulers simultaneously overcomes the other five
and so subdues all the passions.[14]

ST. THEODOROS THE GREAT ASCETIC
II, *A CENTURY OF SPIRITUAL TEXTS*, SEC. 10

Every assent in thought to some forbidden desire, that is, every
submission to self-indulgence, is a sin for a monk. For first the thought
begins to darken the intellect through the passible aspect of the soul,
and then the soul submits to the pleasure, not holding out in the fight.
This is what is called *assent*, which—as has been said—is a sin. When
assent persists, it stimulates the passion in question. Then little by
little it leads to the actual committing of the sin. This is why the
prophet calls blessed those who dash the children of Babylon against
the stones (Psalm 137:9). People with understanding and discretion
will know what is meant.[15]

ST. THEODOROS THE GREAT ASCETIC
II, *A CENTURY OF SPIRITUAL TEXTS*, SEC. 19

16 This sounds very much like the practice of nonattachment, found in Buddhism.

17 Maximos (580–662) was a monk and ascetic who is widely considered to be the greatest of the Byzantine theologians. A great opponent of the Monothelite heresy (which claimed that Jesus had only a divine will, and not a human will as well), he was tortured and died as a result of his defense of Orthodoxy. His theology was a synthesis of what had come before him, and it became a great influence on John of Damaskos, Symeon the New Theologian, and Gregory Palamas.

18 The spiritual tradition takes seriously the warnings of the Epistle of James against the misuse of the tongue. Slander is a misuse of the power of human speech, and Maximos here says it is doubly sinful.

While we are oppressed and imprisoned by the passions, we are often
at a loss to know why we suffer from them. We must, therefore, realize
that it is because we allow ourselves to be diverted from the
contemplation of God that we are taken captive in this way. But if a
man fixes his intellect without distraction on our Master and God,
then the Savior of all can himself be trusted to deliver such a soul from
its impassioned servitude.

ST. THEODOROS THE GREAT ASCETIC
II, A CENTURY OF SPIRITUAL TEXTS, SEC. 90

What an immense struggle it is to break the fetters binding us so
strongly to material things, to stop worshiping these things, and to
acquire instead a state of holiness. Indeed, unless our soul is truly
noble and courageous it cannot embark on such a task. For our goal is
not merely the purification of the passions: this by itself is not real
virtue, but preparation for virtue. To purification from vicious habits
must be added the acquisition of the virtues.[16]

ST. THEODOROS THE GREAT ASCETIC
II, THEORETIKON

A pure soul is one freed from passions and constantly delighted by
divine love. A culpable passion is an impulse from the soul that is
contrary to nature. Dispassion is a peaceful condition of the soul in
which the soul is not easily moved to evil.

ST. MAXIMOS THE CONFESSOR[17]
II, FIRST CENTURY ON LOVE, SEC. 34–36

Silence the man who utters slander in your hearing. Otherwise, you
sin twice over: first, you accustom yourself to this deadly passion and,
second, you fail to prevent him from gossiping against his neighbor.[18]

ST. MAXIMOS THE CONFESSOR
II, FIRST CENTURY ON LOVE, SEC. 60

19 While each of the three aspects or powers of the soul can be attacked by the passions, Maximos suggests that the passions that plague the incensive aspect are the most difficult to combat—passions that often show themselves in the form of anger. Accordingly, God has provided "a stronger remedy"—the commandment to love.

20 While the body is spiritually neutral, if the intellect dwells on concerns of the flesh rather than spiritual pursuits, then it becomes concerned mostly with satisfying carnal needs.

Some passions pertain to the body; others to the soul. The first are occasioned by the body; the second by external objects. Love and self-control overcome both kinds, the first curbing the passions of the soul and the second those of the body. Some passions pertain to the soul's incensive power, and others to its desiring aspect. Both kinds are aroused through the senses. They are aroused when the soul lacks love and self-control. The passions of the soul's incensive power are more difficult to combat than those of its desiring aspect. Consequently, our Lord has given us a stronger remedy against them: the commandment of love. While passions such as ignorance and forgetfulness affect but one of the soul's three aspects—the incensive, the desiring, or the intelligent—listlessness alone seizes control of all the soul's powers and rouses almost all the passions together. This is why this passion is more serious than all the others. Hence, our Lord has given us an excellent remedy against it, saying: "You will gain possession of your souls through your patient endurance" (Luke 21:19).[19]

ST. MAXIMOS THE CONFESSOR
II, *FIRST CENTURY ON LOVE*, SEC. 64–67

If the intellect inclines to God, it treats the body as its servant and provides it with no more than it needs to sustain life. But if it inclines to the flesh, it becomes the servant of the passions and is always thinking about how to fulfill its desires.[20]

ST. MAXIMOS THE CONFESSOR
II, *THIRD CENTURY ON LOVE*, SEC. 12

21 It is common in the *Philokalia* to find very specific "remedies" for particular "ailments." Thus, Maximos here identifies three spiritual illnesses and prescribes three courses of treatment.

+ "[Our] aim is not to eliminate the passions but to redirect their energy. Uncontrolled rage must be turned into righteous indignation, spiteful jealousy into zeal for the truth, sexual lust into an eros that is pure in its fervor. The passions, then, are to be purified, not killed; to be educated, not eradicated; to be used positively, not negatively. To ourselves and to others we say, not 'Suppress,' but 'Transfigure.'"

—Kallistos Ware, *The Orthodox Way*

If you wish to master your thoughts, concentrate on the passions and you will easily drive the thoughts arising from them out of your intellect. With regard to unchastity, for instance, fast and keep vigils, labor, and avoid meeting people. With regard to anger and resentment, be indifferent to fame, dishonor, and material things. With regard to rancor, pray for him who has offended you and you will be delivered.[21]

ST. MAXIMOS THE CONFESSOR
II, *THIRD CENTURY ON LOVE*, SEC. 13

Impurity of soul lies in its not functioning in accordance with nature. It is because of this that impassioned thoughts are produced in the intellect. The soul functions in accordance with nature when its passible aspects—that is, its incensive power and its desire—remain dispassionate in the face of provocations both from things and from the conceptual images of these things.

ST. MAXIMOS THE CONFESSOR
II, *THIRD CENTURY ON LOVE*, SEC. 35

22 While the Fathers sometimes write as if images themselves are what cause spiritual problems, Maximos is more precise, saying here that it is not the images but the passions linked to the images that lead us astray. The fundamentalist religious instinct to require women to cover their bodies so that men may not be led into sin is thus shown to be misguided. The problem is not the woman's appearance, but the passions in the man that link the image to sin.

The intellect of a man who enjoys the love of God does not fight against things or their conceptual images. It battles against the passions that are linked with these images. It does not, for example, fight against a woman or against a man who has offended it, or even against the images it forms of them; but it fights against the passions that are linked with those images. The whole purpose of the monk's warfare against the demons is to separate the passions from conceptual images. Otherwise, he will not be able to look on things dispassionately. A thing, a conceptual image, and a passion are each quite different one from the others. For example, a man, a woman, gold, and so forth are things; a conceptual image is a passion-free thought about one of these things; a passion is mindless affection or indiscriminate hatred for one of these same things. The monk's battle is therefore against passion. An impassioned conceptual image is a thought compounded of passion and a conceptual image. If we separate the passion from the conceptual image, what remains is the passion-free thought. We can make this separation by means of spiritual love and self-control, if only we have the will.[22]

ST. MAXIMOS THE CONFESSOR
II, *THIRD CENTURY ON LOVE*, SEC. 40–43

When you overcome one of the grosser passions, such as gluttony, unchastity, anger, or greed, the thought of self-esteem at once assails you. If you defeat this thought, the thought of pride succeeds it.

ST. MAXIMOS THE CONFESSOR
II, *THIRD CENTURY ON LOVE*, SEC. 59

23 According to Maximos, not all passion is bad. Indeed, he says, "There is need for the blessed passion of holy love." The Orthodox tradition does not shy away from the use of *eros*—the Greek name for sexual love—to speak of God's love for us and our love of God. We see this understanding of erotic or passionate love, for example, in the Hebrew Bible's Song of Songs.

Just as passion-free thought about human beings does not compel the intellect to scorn divine things, so passion-free knowledge of divine things does not fully persuade it to scorn human things. For in this world truth exists in shadows and conjectures. That is why there is need for the blessed passion of holy love, which binds the intellect to spiritual contemplation and persuades it to prefer what is immaterial to what is material, and what is intelligible to what is apprehended by the senses.[23]

ST. MAXIMOS THE CONFESSOR
II, *THIRD CENTURY ON LOVE*, SEC. 67

Do not imagine that you enjoy perfect dispassion when the object arousing your intellect is not present. If, when it is present, you remain unmoved by both the object and the subsequent thought of it, you may be sure that you have entered the realm of dispassion. But even so, do not be overconfident; for virtue, when habitual, kills the passions, but when it is neglected they come to life again.

ST. MAXIMOS THE CONFESSOR
II, *FOURTH CENTURY ON LOVE*, SEC. 54

24 While the moral virtues alone do not merit salvation, they are nonetheless essential to spiritual progress in that they form a "garment of incorruption."

25 In addition to the passion of holy love, Maximos argues that the other passions, which normally impede our spiritual progress, can be directed instead toward our spiritual growth.

A life stained with many faults arising from the passions of the flesh is a soiled garment. For from his mode of life, as if from some garment, each man declares himself to be either righteous or wicked. The righteous man has a holy life as a clean garment; the wicked man has a life soiled with evil actions. Thus a "garment stained by the flesh" (Jude 23) is the inner state and disposition of the soul when its conscience is deformed by the recollection of evil impulses and actions arising from the flesh. When this state or disposition constantly envelops the soul like a garment, it is filled with the stink of the passions. But when the virtues, through the power of the Spirit, are interwoven in accordance with the intelligence, they form a garment of incorruption for the soul: dressed in this, the soul becomes beautiful and resplendent. Conversely, when the passions are interwoven under the influence of the flesh, they form a filthy, soiled garment, which reveals the character of the soul, imposing on it a form and image contrary to the divine.[24]

St. Maximos the Confessor
II, *First Century of Various Texts*, sec. 61

Even the passions become good if we wisely and diligently detach them from what is bodily and direct them toward the acquisition of what is heavenly. This happens, for example, when we turn desire into a noetic yearning for heavenly blessings; or when we turn pleasure into the gentle delight that the volitive energy of the intellect finds in divine gifts; or when we turn fear into protective concern to escape punishments threatening us because of our sins; or when we turn distress into corrective remorse for present sin. In short, the passions become good if—like wise physicians who use the body of the viper as a remedy against present or expected harm resulting from its bite—we use them to destroy present or expected evil, and in order to acquire and safeguard virtue and spiritual knowledge.[25]

St. Maximos the Confessor
II, *First Century of Various Texts*, sec. 66

26   Thalassios was abbot of a monastery in northern Libya in the late-sixth to early-seventh century. He was a friend of Maximos the Confessor, who addressed his longest theological treatise to Thalassios.

27   The West has a tradition of seven deadly sins, which are pride, lust, avarice, gluttony, wrath, envy, and sloth. John's list is essentially the same, although he adds an eighth, self-esteem, which he distinguishes from pride.

Total dispassion renders our conceptual images passion-free: perfect
spiritual knowledge brings us into the presence of him who is utterly
beyond knowledge.

St. Thalassios the Libyan[26]
II, On Love, Self-control and Life in Accordance
with the Intellect, First Century, sec. 73

You should also learn to distinguish the impassioned thoughts that
promote every sin. The thoughts that encompass all evil are eight in
number[27]: gluttony, unchastity, avarice, anger, dejection, listlessness,
self-esteem, and pride. It does not lie within our power to decide
whether or not these eight impassioned thoughts are going to arise
and disturb us. But to dwell on them or not to dwell on them, to excite
the passions or not to excite them, does lie within our power. In this
connection, we should distinguish between seven different terms:
provocation, coupling, passion, wrestling, captivity, assent (which
comes very close to performance), and actualization. Provocation is
simply a suggestion coming from the enemy, like "do this" or "do that,"
such as our Lord himself experienced when he heard the words,
"Command that these stones become bread" (Matthew 4:3). Coupling
is the acceptance of the thought suggested by the enemy. It means
dwelling on the thought and choosing deliberately to dally with it in a
pleasurable manner. Passion is the state resulting from coupling ... it
means letting the imagination brood on the thought continually.
Wrestling is the resistance offered to the impassioned thought....
Captivity is the forcible and compulsive abduction of the heart already
dominated by prepossession and long habit. Assent is giving approval
to the passion inherent in the thought. Actualization is putting the
impassioned thought into effect once it has received our assent. If we
can confront the first of these things, the provocation, in a
dispassionate way, or firmly rebut it at the outset, we thereby cut off at
once everything that comes after.

(continued on page 155)

28 Each specific sin has a specific remedy. Here we see how John distinguishes between pride and self-esteem. The remedy for self-esteem is "doing good in secret" and "praying constantly with a contrite heart." The remedy for pride is refraining from "judging or despising anyone."

29 John of Damaskos (ca. 675–749) was an important theologian best known for his summary of theology titled *On the Orthodox Faith.* Nikodimos attributes to him a summary of the spiritual life that is included in the *Philokalia;* it is titled *On the Virtues and the Vices.* However, it is not likely to be his work or the work of other writers who have been identified as authors—Ephrem the Syrian and Athanasios.

These eight passions should be destroyed as follows[28]: gluttony by self-control; unchastity by desire for God and longing for the blessings held in store; avarice by compassion for the poor; anger by goodwill and love for all men; worldly dejection by spiritual joy; listlessness by patience, perseverance, and offering thanks to God; self-esteem by doing good in secret and by praying constantly with a contrite heart; and pride by not judging or despising anyone in the manner of the boastful Pharisee (Luke 18:11–12), and by considering oneself the least of all men. When the intellect has been freed in this way from the passions we have described and been raised up to God, it will henceforth lead the life of blessedness, receiving the pledge of the Holy Spirit (2 Corinthians 1:22). And when it departs this life, dispassionate and full of true knowledge, it will stand before the light of the Holy Trinity and with the divine angels will shine in glory through all eternity.

St. John of Damaskos[29]
II, *On the Virtues and the Vices*

30 Western Christians typically see sins of the body (such as drunkenness, unchastity, adultery, and theft) as more weighty, more sinful than sins of the soul. But John says this is a serious error, for the passions of the soul (such as envy, rancor, malice, insensitivity, and avarice) "are much worse and much more serious than bodily passions."

There is something else that you must know if you really want to attain virtue and avoid sin. Just as the soul is incomparably better than the body and in many major respects is altogether more excellent and precious, so the virtues of the soul are infinitely superior to the virtues of the body. This is especially true of those virtues that imitate God and bear his name. Conversely, the vices of the soul are much worse than the passions of the body, both in the actions they produce and in the punishments they incur. I do not know why, but most people overlook this fact. They treat drunkenness, unchastity, adultery, theft, and all such vices with great concern, avoiding them or punishing them as something whose very appearance is loathsome to most men. But the passions of the soul are much worse and much more serious than bodily passions. For they degrade men to the level of demons and lead them, insensible as they are, to the eternal punishment reserved for all who obstinately cling to such vices. These passions of the soul are envy, rancor, malice, insensitivity, avarice—which according to the apostle is the root of all evil (1 Timothy 6:10)—and all vices of a similar nature.[30]

ST. JOHN OF DAMASKOS
II, *ON THE VIRTUES AND THE VICES*

The impassioned man is strongly prone to sin in thought, even though, for the time being, he does not sin outwardly. The self-indulgent man actually commits the sin suggested in thought, even though he suffers inwardly. The man of impassioned craving is given over freely or, rather, servilely, to the various modes of sinning. The dispassionate man is not dominated by any of these degrees of passion. Passionateness is removed from the soul through fasting and prayer; self-indulgence through vigil and silence; and impassioned craving through stillness and attentiveness. Dispassion is established through remembrance of God.

ILIAS THE PRESBYTER
III, *GNOMIC ANTHOLOGY I*, SEC. 73–74

31 In accordance with what John of Damaskos said above, Ilias reminds us that the bodily passions and sins are less serious than the soul's passions and sins. While he characterizes the former as wild animals and the latter as birds, he points out that it is much more difficult to get rid of the birds than it is the wild animals.

32 While *theosis*, or deification, is treated in chapter 7, Peter notes here that becoming dispassionate is a necessary prerequisite to being deified.

33 Peter of Damaskos (twelfth century?) is second only to Maximos the Confessor in the amount of his writing included in the *Philokalia*, yet nothing is known of him outside of his writings. We may infer from his writings that he was a monk, and from his selection of writers we can deduce that he belonged to the spiritual tradition associated with Evagrios and Maximos the Confessor.

Bodily passions are like wild animals, while passions of the soul are like birds. The man engaged in ascetic practice can keep the animals out of the noetic vineyard; but unless he enters into a state of spiritual contemplation, he cannot keep the birds away, however much he strives to guard himself inwardly.[31]

ILIAS THE PRESBYTER
III, GNOMIC ANTHOLOGY IV, SEC. 59

Those who indulge their passions, being materially minded, are distracted during prayer by their thoughts as by frogs. Those who restrain their passions are gladdened during prayer by the changing forms of contemplation, which are like nightingales moving from one branch to another. But in the dispassionate there is silence and great quiescence of both thought and intellection during prayer.

ILIAS THE PRESBYTER
III, GNOMIC ANTHOLOGY IV, SEC. 76

Through the wisdom and the indwelling of the Holy Spirit and through adoption to sonship, we are crucified with Christ and buried with him, and we rise with him and ascend with him spiritually by imitating his way of life in this world. To speak simply, we become gods by adoption through grace, receiving the pledge of eternal blessedness, as St. Gregory the Theologian says. In this way, with regard to the eight evil thoughts, we become dispassionate, just, good, and wise, having God within ourselves—as Christ himself has told us (John 14:21–23)—through the keeping of the commandments in order, from the first to the last.[32]

ST. PETER OF DAMASKOS[33]
III, A TREASURY OF DIVINE KNOWLEDGE, INTRODUCTION

34 This follows the analysis of virtue given by Aristotle (384–322 BCE) in his *Nicomachean Ethics*. Aristotle says that a virtue lies in the mean between an excess and a deficiency of a given kind of action or thinking. These extremes are vices. For example, courage lies between the excess of foolhardiness and the deficiency of cowardice.

35 John the Evangelist is known in the East as John the Theologian, a title that is probably the basis of the English title John the Divine. Only two other saints in the Orthodox Church are given this title: Gregory (of Nazianzus) the Theologian and Symeon the New Theologian.

Each virtue lies between two unnatural passions. Moral judgment lies between craftiness and thoughtlessness; self-restraint, between obduracy and licentiousness; courage, between overbearingness and cowardice; justice between overfrugality and greed. The four virtues constitute an image of the heavenly man, while the eight unnatural passions constitute an image of the earthly man (1 Corinthians 15:49).[34]

ST. PETER OF DAMASKOS
III, *A TREASURY OF DIVINE KNOWLEDGE*,
THE FOUR VIRTUES OF THE SOUL

In a similar way each of us faithful is attacked and led astray by the passions; but if he is at peace with God and with his neighbor he overcomes them all. These passions are the "world" that St. John the Theologian[35] told us to hate (1 John 2:15), meaning that we are to hate, not God's creatures, but worldly desires. The soul is at peace with God when it is at peace with itself and has become wholly deiform. It is also at peace with God when it is at peace with all men, even if it suffers terrible things at their hands. Because of its forbearance it is not perturbed, but bears all things (1 Corinthians 13:7), wishes good to all, loves all, both for God's sake and for the sake of their own nature.

ST. PETER OF DAMASKOS
III, *A TREASURY OF DIVINE KNOWLEDGE*, BOOK 2.24 JOY

+ "Thus the saints, who underwent great discipline to control their
feelings and labored in mental prayer in the vineyard of their own heart
and purified their mind of all passions, have discovered the Lord and
attained spiritual wisdom. We, too, who are so enflamed by the fires of
our passions, are enjoined to draw the living water from the fountain of
the Sacred Scriptures, which have the power to extinguish the fires
of our passion and instruct us in the understanding of the truth."

—St. Nil Sorsky,
Nil Sorsky: The Complete Writings

The genuine and perfected Christian … with great enjoyment and spiritual pleasure participates effortlessly and without impediment in all the virtues and all the supernatural fruits of the Spirit—love, peace, patient endurance, faith, humility, and the entire truly golden galaxy of virtue—as though they were natural. He does not fight any longer against the passions of evil, for he has been totally set free of them by the Lord; while from the blessed Spirit he has received Christ's perfect peace and joy in his heart. Of such a man it may be said that he cleaves to the Lord and has become one spirit with him (1 Corinthians 6:17).

ST. MAKARIOS OF EGYPT
III, *PRAYER*, SEC. 23

Passions acted out can be cured by action. Dissipation, sensuality, gluttony, and a dissolute, profligate life produce a passion-charged state of soul and impel it to unnatural actions. On the other hand, restraint and self-control, ascetic labor, and spiritual struggle translate the soul from its passion-charged state to a state of dispassion.

NIKITAS STITHATOS
IV, *ON THE PRACTICE OF THE VIRTUES: ONE HUNDRED TEXTS*, SEC. 34

1 Although Symeon the New Theologian quotes the already old saying that "your cell can teach you everything," Evagrios says that the cell itself may also become a distraction. For him, the chief criterion "for testing the value of everything" is stillness (*hesychia*).

2 Because the human being is a psychosomatic unity, stillness of the body is necessary in order to achieve inner stillness.

3 Love is always the foundational commandment and gift, but in order to maintain it, both stillness and detachment from things are very important.

6 □ Stillness

If you find yourself growing strongly attached to your cell, leave it, do not cling to it, be ruthless. Do everything possible to attain stillness and freedom from distraction, and struggle to live according to God's will, battling against invisible enemies. If you cannot attain stillness where you now live, consider living in exile, and try to make up your mind and go. Be like an astute businessman: make stillness your criterion for testing the value of everything, and choose always what contributes to it.[1]

EVAGRIOS THE SOLITARY
I, ON ASCETICISM AND STILLNESS

He who wants to cross the spiritual sea is long-suffering, humble, vigilant, and self-controlled. If he impetuously embarks on it without these four virtues, he agitates his heart, but cannot cross. Stillness helps us by making evil inoperative. If it also takes to itself these four virtues in prayer, it is the most direct support in attaining dispassion. The intellect cannot be still unless the body is still also; and the wall between them cannot be demolished without stillness and prayer.[2]

ST. MARK THE ASCETIC
I, ON THOSE WHO THINK THEY ARE MADE
RIGHTEOUS BY WORKS, SEC. 29–31

Of all the commandments, therefore, the most comprehensive is to love God and our neighbor. This love is made firm through abstaining from physical things, and through stillness of thought.[3]

ST. MARK THE ASCETIC
I, ON THOSE WHO THINK THEY ARE MADE
RIGHTEOUS BY WORKS, SEC. 223

+ "Silence is a mystery of the world to come."

—St. Isaac of Syria, *Light through Darkness: The Orthodox Tradition*

4 Hesychios understands stillness as the "mother of all the virtues," and the Jesus Prayer as the surest path to achieving stillness. The "wise man" is likely a reference to John Klimakos.

Attentiveness is the heart's stillness, unbroken by any thought. In this
stillness the heart breathes and invokes, endlessly and without ceasing,
only Jesus Christ, who is the Son of God and himself God.

St. Hesychios the Priest
I, On Watchfulness and Holiness, sec. 5

Let your model for stillness of heart be the man who holds a mirror
into which he looks. Then you will see both good and evil imprinted
on your heart.

St. Hesychios the Priest
I, On Watchfulness and Holiness, sec. 48

That great spiritual master David said to the Lord: "I shall preserve my
strength through Thee" (Psalm 59:9, LXX). So the strength of the
heart's stillness, mother of all the virtues, is preserved in us through our
being helped by the Lord. For he has given us the commandments,
and when we call upon him constantly he expels from us that foul
forgetfulness that destroys the heart's stillness as water destroys fire.
Therefore, monk, do not "sleep unto death" (Psalm 13:3, LXX) because
of your negligence; but lash the enemy with the name of Jesus and, as
a certain wise man has said, let the name of Jesus adhere to your
breath, and then you will know the blessings of stillness.**4**

St. Hesychios the Priest
I, On Watchfulness and Holiness, sec. 100

We should try to preserve the precious gifts that preserve us from evil,
whether on the plane of the senses or on that of the intellect. These
gifts are the guarding of the intellect with the invocation of Jesus
Christ, continuous insight into the heart's depths, stillness of mind
unbroken even by thoughts that appear to be good, and the capacity
to be empty of all thought. In this way the demons will not steal in
undetected; and if we suffer pain through remaining centered in the
heart, consolation is at hand.

St. Hesychios the Priest
I, On Watchfulness and Holiness, sec. 103

5 To be a true monk, one must first resolve to be a monk, and by this Hesychios means one must be determined to practice "perfect stillness."

6 The new monk who has "only recently escaped from the agitation of the world" is particularly susceptible to being plagued by old fantasies and the formation of new ones. The antidote to these distractions is the practice of stillness. In our own lives we can be distracted from prayer by the concerns of the world and can practice stillness as well.

If you wish to be "in the Lord," do not just *seem* to be a monk, and good, and gentle, and always at one with God; decide to *be* such a person in truth. With all your strength, pursue the virtue of attentiveness—that guard and watch of the intellect, that perfect stillness of heart and blessed state of the soul when free from images, which is all too rarely found in man.[5]

ST. HESYCHIOS THE PRIEST
I, ON WATCHFULNESS AND HOLINESS, SEC. 115

Those who have only recently escaped from the agitation of the world should be advised to practice stillness; otherwise, by frequently going out, they will reopen the wounds inflicted on their mind through the senses. They should take care not to add new images to their old fantasies. Those who have only just renounced the world find stillness hard to practice, for memory now has time to stir up all the filth that is within them, whereas previously it had no chance to do this because of their many preoccupations. But, though hard to practice, stillness will in time free the intellect from being disturbed by impure thoughts. Since the aim is to cleanse the soul and purify it from all defilement, such people should avoid everything that makes the soul unclean. They should keep their intelligence in a state of profound calm, far from all that irritates it, and should refrain from talking with men of frivolous character. They should embrace solitude, the mother of wisdom.[6]

ST. NEILOS THE ASCETIC
I, ASCETIC DISCOURSE

Spiritual knowledge comes through prayer, deep stillness, and complete detachment, while wisdom comes through humble meditation on Holy Scripture and, above all, through grace given by God.

ST. DIADOCHOS OF PHOTIKI
I, ON SPIRITUAL KNOWLEDGE, SEC. 9

7 Monks should not spend much time outside of their cells, as this is likely to lead to spending too much time with other people. Such social intercourse would undoubtedly disturb the monks' practice of stillness.

8 Although the monk should not seek out the company of others, the monk should nevertheless welcome visits from fellow monks and not view these visits as distractions. This would include pilgrims seeking spiritual counsel. The law of love and hospitality trumps even the importance of stillness for the monk.

You must avoid continuously wasting time outside your cell, if you have indeed chosen to practice stillness. For it is most harmful, depriving you of grace, darkening your mind, and sapping your aspiration. That is why it is said: "Restlessness of desire perverts the guileless intellect" (Wisdom 4:12). So restrict your relationships with other people, lest your intellect should become distracted and your life of stillness disrupted.[7]

St. Theodoros the Great Ascetic
II, *A Century of Spiritual Texts*, sec. 56

When we receive visits from our brethren, we should not consider this an irksome interruption of our stillness, lest we cut ourselves off from the law of love. Nor should we receive them as if we were doing them a favor, but rather as if it is we ourselves who were receiving a favor; and because we are indebted to them, we should beg them cheerfully to enjoy our hospitality, as the patriarch Abraham has shown us. This is why St. John, too, says: "My children, let us love not in word or tongue, but in action and truth. And by this we know that we belong to the truth" (1 John 3:18–19).[8]

St. Theodoros the Great Ascetic
II, *A Century of Spiritual Texts*, sec. 84

Stillness, prayer, love, and self-control are a four-horsed chariot bearing the intellect to heaven.

St. Thalassios the Libyan
II, *On Love, Self-control, and Life in Accordance with the Intellect*, First Century, sec. 24

Stillness and prayer are the greatest weapons of virtue, for they purify the intellect and confer on it spiritual insight.

St. Thalassios the Libyan
II, *On Love, Self-control, and Life in Accordance with the Intellect*, First Century, sec. 67

9 Distraction will come from images, and images from our five senses. It is therefore important to guard the senses through the practice of stillness.

10 Desire is difficult to control. Thalassios indicates that while self-control and strenuous effort can check desire, we must practice stillness and intense longing for God if we are to eradicate it.

11 Abba Philimon (sixth or seventh century?) is unknown except for the narrative that is included in the *Philokalia,* which identifies him as an Egyptian priest. He is the first person to give what is now the usual form of the Jesus Prayer—"Lord Jesus Christ, Son of God, have mercy on me."

Enclose your senses in the citadel of stillness so that they do not
involve the intellect in their desires.[9]

ST. THALASSIOS THE LIBYAN
II, ON LOVE, SELF-CONTROL, AND LIFE IN ACCORDANCE
WITH THE INTELLECT, SECOND CENTURY, SEC. 10

Self-control and strenuous effort curb desire; stillness and intense
longing for God wither it.[10]

ST. THALASSIOS THE LIBYAN
II, ON LOVE, SELF-CONTROL, AND LIFE IN ACCORDANCE
WITH THE INTELLECT, SECOND CENTURY, SEC. 21

The forceful practice of self-control and love, patience and stillness,
will destroy the passions hidden within us.

ST. THALASSIOS THE LIBYAN
II, ON LOVE, SELF-CONTROL, AND LIFE IN ACCORDANCE
WITH THE INTELLECT, THIRD CENTURY, SEC. 8

Philimon knew that Paulinos, too, aspired to the [eremitical] state; and
with this in mind he implanted in him teachings taken from Scripture
and the Fathers that emphasized, as Moses had done, how impossible
it is to conform to God without complete stillness; how stillness gives
birth to ascetic effort, ascetic effort to tears, tears to awe, awe to
humility, humility to foresight, foresight to love; and how love restores
the soul to health and makes it dispassionate, so that one then knows
that one is not far from God.

ABBA PHILIMON[11]
II, A DISCOURSE ON ABBA PHILIMON

The only path leading to heaven is that of complete stillness, the
avoidance of all evil, the acquisition of blessings, perfect love toward
God, and communion with him in holiness and righteousness. If a man
has attained these things, he will soon ascend to the heavenly realm.

ABBA PHILIMON
II, A DISCOURSE ON ABBA PHILIMON

12 Progress in the spiritual life does not eliminate suffering, but the practice of stillness allows us to find meaning in it.

13 These words were heard by the Desert Father Abba Arsenius (ca. 360–449).

Enduring a great number of trials while dwelling in extreme stillness in solitary places, I was much tempted and suffered greatly. But nothing is to be gained by speaking of such bitter things to people who as yet have no experience of stillness. When tempted, I always did this: I put all my hope in God, for it was to him that I made my vows of renunciation. And he at once delivered me from all of my distress. Because of this, brother, I no longer take thought for myself. I know that he takes thought for me, and so I bear more lightly the trials that come upon me. The only thing I offer from myself is unceasing prayer. I know that the more the suffering, the greater the reward for him who endures it. It is a means to reconciliation with the righteous Judge.[12]

ABBA PHILIMON
II, *A DISCOURSE ON ABBA PHILIMON*

It is very rare to find people whose intelligence is in a state of stillness. Indeed, such a state is only to be found in those who through their whole manner of life strive to attract divine grace and blessing to themselves.

ST. PHILOTHEOS OF SINAI
III, *FORTY TEXTS ON WATCHFULNESS*, SEC. 3

Stillness, which is the basis of the soul's purification, makes the observance of the commandments relatively painless. "Flee," it has been said, "keep silence, be still, for herein lie the roots of sinlessness."[13] Again it has been said: "Flee men and you will be saved." For human society does not permit the intellect to perceive either its own faults or the wiles of the demons, so as to guard itself against them. Nor, on the other hand, does it allow the intellect to perceive God's providence and bounty, so as to acquire in this way knowledge of God and humility.

ST. PETER OF DAMASKOS
III, *A TREASURY OF DIVINE KNOWLEDGE*, INTRODUCTION

+ "Blessed is the person who seriously meditates on the Writings of the Spirit-filled Fathers and follows their teachings and examples. Such a person is completely taken up with this prayer [of the heart] and is able to overcome always every kind of thought, not only an evil one, but also one that seemingly is a good one. And in this manner, he attains perfect silence even in his thoughts, for the prayer is the peak and crown of all ascetical practices. For Symeon the New Theologian teaches that true silence and tranquility (*hesychia*) is to seek the Lord in the heart, that is, to push the mind into the heart consciously and to pray and be concerned only with this."

—St. Nil Sorsky,
Nil Sorsky: The Complete Writings

The first of these seven forms of discipline consists in stillness, or in living a life without distraction, far from all worldly care. By removing ourselves from human society and distraction, we escape from turmoil and from him who "walks about like a roaring lion, seeking whom he may devour" (1 Peter 5:8) through idle talk and the worries of life.

ST. PETER OF DAMASKOS
III, *A TREASURY OF DIVINE KNOWLEDGE*,
THE SEVEN FORMS OF BODILY DISCIPLINE

Blessed are they who are completely devoted to God, either through obedience to someone experienced in the practice of the virtues and living an ordered life in stillness, or else through themselves living in stillness and total detachment, scrupulously obedient to God's will, and seeking the advice of experienced men in everything they say or think. Blessed above all are those who seek to attain dispassion and spiritual knowledge unlaboriously through their total devotion to God: as God himself has said through his prophet, "Devote yourselves to stillness and know that I am God" (Psalm 46:10).

ST. PETER OF DAMASKOS
III, *A TREASURY OF DIVINE KNOWLEDGE*, THE BODILY VIRTUES AS
TOOLS FOR THE ACQUISITION OF THE VIRTUES OF THE SOUL

14 The monk is to "seek his own soul" through the prayerful reading of the Bible. This reading is not chiefly an academic, historical, or dogmatic study. The monk approaches the Bible as a spiritual guidebook.

15 A common mistake in the spiritual life is to ignore our weaknesses and focus instead on our strengths. However, such ignorance is dangerous in the spiritual life. Since the Fathers understand sin as a medical model, it is necessary to get a complete and accurate diagnosis of our spiritual illnesses if we are to know how best to treat them.

If we want to perceive our lethal condition, we must abandon our own desires and all the preoccupations of this life. Through this flight from everything, let us assiduously devote ourselves to God with a devotion that is truly blessed and divine. Let each of us seek his own soul through studying the divine Scriptures, either in perfect obedience of soul and body or in stillness following the angelic way. This is especially important for those who are as yet subject to the passions and cannot control their own desires, whether great or small. "Sit in your own cell," it has been said, "and your cell will teach you all things." Or as St. Basil puts it, "Stillness initiates the soul's purification." It is also true that Solomon says, "God has given noxious distraction to the sons of men, so that they may be distracted by vain things" (Ecclesiastes 1:13). This is to prevent their mindless and impassioned inertia from dragging them down into what is even worse.[14]

St. Peter of Damaskos
III, *A Treasury of Divine Knowledge*, Obedience and Stillness

Nothing so benefits the weak as withdrawal into stillness, or the man subject to the passions and without spiritual knowledge as obedience combined with stillness. Nor is there anything better than to know one's own weakness and ignorance, nor anything worse than not to recognize them.[15]

St. Peter of Damaskos
III, *A Treasury of Divine Knowledge*,
That We Should Not Despair Even If We Sin Many Times

16 While it is often acknowledged that God has given revelation through both the Bible and nature, the tradition of the *Philokalia* teaches that neither are "open" books that may be easily understood. Peter here refers to the mysteries that are hidden in Scripture and creation. A mystery is something whose meaning is revealed by God to someone who enters into and experiences it. Therefore, to understand the Bible or nature we must undertake the spiritual journey, including the practice of stillness and devotion.

Stillness and withdrawal from men and human affairs are of benefit to all, but especially to those who are weak and subject to the passions. For the intellect alone cannot obtain dispassion by means of ascetic practice alone; such practice must be followed by spiritual contemplation. Nor will anyone escape unharmed from distraction and from exercising authority over others unless he has first acquired dispassion through withdrawal. The cares and confusion of this life are liable to harm even the perfect and the dispassionate.

ST. PETER OF DAMASKOS
III, *A TREASURY OF DIVINE KNOWLEDGE*,
THAT STILLNESS IS OF GREAT BENEFIT TO THOSE SUBJECT TO PASSION

We must remember, too, that stillness is the highest gift of all, and that without it we cannot be purified and come to know our weakness and the trickery of the demons; neither will we be able to understand the power of God and his providence from the divine words that we read and sing. For we all need this devotion and stillness, total or partial, if we are to attain the humility and spiritual knowledge necessary for the understanding of the mysteries hidden in the divine Scriptures and in all creation.[16]

ST. PETER OF DAMASKOS
III, *A TREASURY OF DIVINE KNOWLEDGE*, SPURIOUS KNOWLEDGE

St. Prochoros says of St. John the Evangelist that he did not wish to leave his beloved stillness, even though as an apostle he was under obligation to renounce the stillness and to proclaim the Gospel. It was not in the least because he was subject to the passions that St. John took refuge in stillness, for he of all men was most free of them. He did so because he did not want ever to be cut off from the contemplation of God or to be deprived of the great sweetness of stillness.

ST. PETER OF DAMASKOS
III, *A TREASURY OF DIVINE KNOWLEDGE*, SPURIOUS KNOWLEDGE

17 Symeon mentions several different approaches used by different Fathers, and he does not say here that one is better than another. He does, however, point out that all the techniques he mentions have to do with working on the heart. This is essential for making progress in the spiritual life.

+ "Athos, mountain of silence!"

—Philip Sherrard, *Light through Darkness: The Orthodox Tradition*

Some of the Fathers have called this practice stillness of the heart, others attentiveness, others the guarding of the heart, others watchfulness and rebuttal, and still others the investigation of thoughts and the guarding of the intellect. But all of them alike worked the earth of their own heart, and in this way they were fed on the divine manna (Exodus 16:15).[17]

ST. SYMEON THE NEW THEOLOGIAN
IV, *THE THREE METHODS OF PRAYER*,
THE THIRD METHOD OF PRAYER

Stillness is an undisturbed state of the intellect, the calm of a free and joyful soul, the tranquil unwavering stability of the heart in God, the contemplation of light, the knowledge of the mysteries of God, consciousness of wisdom by virtue of a pure mind, the abyss of divine intellections, the rapture of the intellect, intercourse with God, an unsleeping watchfulness, spiritual prayer, untroubled repose in the midst of great hardship, and, finally, solidarity and union with God.

NIKITAS STITHATOS
IV, *ON THE INNER NATURE OF THINGS AND
ON THE PURIFICATION OF THE INTELLECT*, SEC. 64

If you generate the honey of the virtues in stillness, you will through struggle and self-discipline transcend the lowly condition of man's fallen state and by overcoming your presumption you will restore the soul's powers to their natural state.

NIKITAS STITHATOS
IV, *ON THE INNER NATURE OF THINGS AND
ON THE PURIFICATION OF THE INTELLECT*, SEC. 66

18 Nikitas puts forth the acid test for the hesychast, the follower of the path of stillness. If he has not obtained the "holy and godlike state of perfection," then he has not achieved stillness and therefore has not yet become a true hesychast.

19 Nikiphoros the Monk (thirteenth century) was a Roman Catholic from Italy who, upon traveling to the Byzantine Empire, confessed the Orthodox faith and became a monk on Mount Athos. In his writings he is particularly concerned with addressing how we can use our bodies to aid us in prayer.

20 Gregory (ca. 1265–1346) was a great ascetic and monk of the Monastery of St. Catherine on Mount Sinai, which has been in operation since the sixth century. He brought from Sinai the discipline of the invocation of the name of Jesus, combined with breathing techniques. He is seen as the person most responsible for the renewal of Orthodox monasticism, hesychastic tradition, and the practice of the Jesus Prayer in the fourteenth and fifteenth centuries.

It is stillness, full of wisdom and benediction, that leads us to this holy and godlike state of perfection—when, that is, it is practiced and pursued genuinely. If an apparent hesychast has not obtained this eminence and perfection, his stillness is still not yet this noetic and perfect stillness. Indeed, until he has obtained this eminence, he will not have even stilled the inner turbulence of the anarchic passions.[18]

NIKITAS STITHATOS
IV, *ON SPIRITUAL KNOWLEDGE*, SEC. 25

Assimilation to God, conferred upon us through intense purification and deep love for God, can be maintained only through an unceasing aspiration toward him on the part of the contemplative intellect. Such aspiration is born within the soul through the persistent stillness produced by the acquisition of the virtues, by ceaseless and undistracted spiritual prayer, by total self-control, and by intensive reading of the Scriptures.

NIKITAS STITHATOS
IV, *ON SPIRITUAL KNOWLEDGE*, SEC. 35

Some of the saints have called attentiveness the guarding of the intellect; others have called it custody of the heart, or watchfulness, or noetic stillness, and others something else. All these expressions indicate one and the same thing, just as *bread* and *a round* or *a slice* do; and you should read them in this sense.[19]

NIKIPHOROS THE MONK
IV, *ON WATCHFULNESS*, FROM NIKIPHOROS HIMSELF

Christ is the capstone (Ephesians 2:20) uniting us with himself. He is the pearl of great price (Matthew 13:46): it is this the monk seeks when he plunges into the depths of stillness and it is this for which he sells all his own desires through obedience to the commandments, so that he may acquire it even in this life.

ST. GREGORY OF SINAI[20]
IV, *ON COMMANDMENTS AND DOCTRINES*, SEC. 83

21 The great religious traditions all begin with the requirement of obedience, usually to the commands of God or moral prescriptions and
proscriptions. It is key to the spiritual life. In the Orthodox Christian tradition, those seeking spiritual progress and illumination usually place
themselves under the guidance of a spiritual father or mother to whom
they promise their obedience, confident that such progress and illumination will be found first and foremost because of their commitment
to obey.

22 Once again, only someone who has achieved holiness is in a position
to interpret the Scriptures. This, of course, does not invalidate the work
of biblical scholars or the merits of the personal study of the Scriptures. But for the Fathers of the *Philokalia,* the deepest meaning of
the Bible is its spiritual guidance for achieving holiness.

23 See chapter 3, note 5. *Theology,* as understood in the East, is meant
to be transformative. It has been said that Western Christians go to
church to learn about God, whereas Eastern Christians go to church to
kiss God. (One of the Greek words for worship, *proskuneo,* means
"to kiss.")

If you are feeble in practicing the commandments yet want to expel your inner murkiness, the best and most efficient physic is trustful, unhesitating obedience in all things. This remedy, distilled from many virtues, restores vitality and acts like a knife that at a single stroke cuts away festering sores. If, then, in total trust and simplicity, you choose this remedy out of all alternatives, you excise every passion at once. Not only will you reach the state of stillness, but also, through your obedience, you will fully enter into it, having found Christ and become his imitator and servitor in name and act.[21]

ST. GREGORY OF SINAI
IV, *ON COMMANDMENTS AND DOCTRINES*, SEC. 107

An interpreter of sacred texts adept in the mysteries of the kingdom of God is everyone who after practicing the ascetic life devotes himself to the contemplation of God and cleaves to stillness. Out of the treasury of his heart he brings forth things new and old (Matthew 13:52), that is, things from the Gospel of Christ and the Prophets, or from the New and Old Testaments, or doctrinal teachings and rules of ascetic practice, or themes from the Apostles and from the Law. These are the mysteries new and old that the skilled interpreter brings forth when he has been schooled in the life of holiness.[22]

ST. GREGORY OF SINAI
IV, *ON COMMANDMENTS AND DOCTRINES*, SEC. 127

Stillness gives birth to contemplation, contemplation to spiritual knowledge, and knowledge to the apprehension of the mysteries. The consummation of the mysteries is theology, the fruit of theology is perfect love, of love humility, of humility dispassion, and of dispassion foresight, prophecy and foreknowledge.[23]

ST. GREGORY OF SINAI
IV. *FURTHER TEXTS*, SEC. 5

24 Just as some Fathers identified three primary demons that assail the monk in his spiritual struggle, Gregory identifies three primary virtues that are essential for stillness—self-control, silence, and self-reproach (humility).

+ "*Hesychia* [stillness] signifies concentration combined with inner tranquility. It is not merely to be understood in a negative sense as the absence of speech and outward activity, but it denotes in a positive way the openness of the human heart towards God's love."

—Kallistos Ware, *The Orthodox Way*

St. John Klimakos explicitly says that to attain the state of stillness entails, first, total detachment; second, resolute prayer—this means standing and psalmodizing; and third, unbroken labor of the heart, that is to say, sitting down to pray in stillness.

ST. GREGORY OF SINAI
IV, *ON STILLNESS*, SEC. 4

There are three virtues connected with stillness that we must guard scrupulously, examining ourselves every hour to make sure that we possess them, in case through unmindfulness we are robbed of them and wander far away from them. These virtues are self-control, silence, and self-reproach, which is the same thing as humility. They are all-embracing and support one another; from them prayer is born and through them it burgeons.[24]

ST. GREGORY OF SINAI
IV, *ON PRAYER*, SEC. 7

1   This saying is virtually identical to the earlier formulations of Irenaeus of Lyons in the second century and Athanasios of Alexandria in the fourth century. Irenaeus said that God "became what we are in order to make us what he is"; Athanasios said that "God became man in order that we may become gods." All three authors are giving voice to the Eastern teaching that the entire purpose of the Incarnation (God taking on human nature in the person of Jesus) was the *theosis,* or deification, of human beings. *Logos* ("Word") is a term for Jesus used most famously in the opening chapter of the Gospel of John.

7 □ In the End: Theosis

When we were in this harsh captivity, ruled by invisible and bitter death, the Master of all visible and invisible creation was not ashamed to humble himself and to take upon himself our human nature, subject as it was to the passions of shame and desire and condemned by divine judgment; and he became like us in all things except that he was without sin (Hebrews 4:15), that is, without ignoble passions. All the penalties imposed by divine judgment upon man for the sin of the first transgression—death, toil, hunger, thirst, and the like—he took upon himself, becoming what we are, so that we might become what he is. The Logos became man, so that man might become Logos.[1] Being rich, he became poor for our sake, so that through his poverty we might become rich (2 Corinthians 8:9). In his great love for man he became like us, so that through every virtue we might become like him.

ST. MARK THE ASCETIC
I, *LETTER TO NICOLAS THE SOLITARY*

2 Antony says that God made the rest of creation for the purpose of our deification. Thus, all of creation was meant by God to be a means for our communion with God. But since humanity has instead exploited creation, it has ceased to be a means of communion with God. The Church's mysteries (sacraments) are a return to God's purposes. When water is used in baptism, the original, life-giving purpose of water is recalled. When bread and wine are used in the Eucharist, we are reminded that all meals are meant to be occasions of communion with God.

3 The book of Genesis reports God as saying, "Let us make man in our image, according to our likeness" (Genesis 1:26). Scriptural scholars today see the terms *image* and *likeness* as an instance of parallelism, a poetic way of saying the same thing twice. But the Church Fathers see an important difference between the terms. They say that we are made in the image of God, and our vocation is to grow into God's likeness. Thus, the terms are understood as referring to our potential and its realization; image is to likeness as the acorn is to the oak tree. We can never lose the image of God in which we were created, but through sinful choices we may fail to realize the likeness or even watch it vanish once it is obtained.

All these passions pertain to materiality; yet there was no need for
God to extirpate matter. He has, however, extirpated evil from men for
their own good, by granting them intellect, understanding, spiritual
knowledge, and the power to discern what is good, so that, realizing
the harm that comes from evil, they may avoid it. But the fool pursues
evil and is proud of doing so: he is like someone caught in a snare who
struggles helplessly in its toils. So he is never able to look up, and to
see and know God, who has created all things that man may be saved
and deified.[2]

ST. ANTONY THE GREAT
I, ON THE CHARACTER OF MEN AND ON THE VIRTUOUS LIFE, SEC. 168

When the intellect begins to perceive the Holy Spirit with full
consciousness, we should realize that grace is beginning to paint the
divine likeness over the divine image in us. Artists first draw the
outline of a man in monochrome, and then add one color after
another, until little by little they capture the likeness of their subject
down to the smallest details. In the same way the grace of God starts
by remaking the divine image in man into what it was when he was
first created. But when it sees us longing with all our heart for the
beauty of the divine likeness and humbly standing naked in its atelier,
then by making one virtue after another come into flower and exalting
the beauty of the soul "from glory to glory" (2 Corinthians 3:18), it
depicts the divine likeness on the soul.... Only when it has been made
like God—insofar, of course, as this is possible—does it bear the
divine likeness of love as well. In portraiture, when the full range of
colors is added to the outline, the painter captures the likeness of the
subject, even down to the smile. Something similar happens to those
who are being repainted by God's grace in the divine likeness: when
the luminosity of love is added, then it is evident that the image has
been fully transformed into the beauty of the likeness.[3]

ST. DIADOCHOS OF PHOTIKI
I, ON SPIRITUAL KNOWLEDGE AND DISCRIMINATION, SEC. 89

4 Deification involves the whole person, so it therefore includes the three powers or aspects of the soul as well.

+ "Nothing can separate human nature from God. That is why now, after the Incarnation of the Lord—as much as we, being human may commit sins, as much as we may depart from God—if in repentance we want to unite with him again, we can do so. We can unite with him, become gods by Grace."

—Archimandrite George, *The Deification as the Purpose of Man's Life*

One must first deny oneself and then, taking up the cross, must follow the Master toward the supreme state of deification. What are ascent and deification? For the intellect, they are perfect knowledge of created things, and of him who is above created things, as far as such knowledge is accessible to human nature. For the will, they are total and continuous striving toward primal goodness. And for the incensive power, they are energetic and effective impulsion toward the object of aspiration, persistent, relentless, and unarrested by any practical difficulties, pressing forward impetuously and undeviatingly.**4**

St. Theodoros the Great Ascetic
I, Theoretikon

Everything must be understood in terms of its purpose. It is this that determines the division of everything into its constituent parts, as well as the mutual relationship of those parts. Now the purpose of our life is blessedness or, what is the same thing, the kingdom of heaven or of God. This is not only to behold the Trinity, supreme in kingship, but also to receive an influx of the divine and, as it were, to suffer deification; for by this influx what is lacking and imperfect in us is supplied and perfected.

St. Theodoros the Great Ascetic
I, Theoretikon

5 Maximos is saying that the soul is not eternal in the sense that God is—that is, not having any beginning. The soul has a beginning in that God creates it in time. But through the Resurrection, Jesus Christ has vanquished death for all time and so all souls, once created, are immortal. In the words of the hymn at Pascha (Easter): "Christ is risen from the dead, trampling down death by death, and upon those in the tomb bestowing life!"

When God brought into being natures endowed with intelligence and intellect, he communicated to them, in his supreme goodness, four of the divine attributes by which he sustains, protects, and preserves created things. These attributes are being, eternal being, goodness, and wisdom. Of the four, he granted the first two—being and eternal being—to their essence, and the second two—goodness and wisdom—to their volitive faculty, so that what he is in his essence the creature may become by participation. This is why man is said to have been created in the image and likeness of God (Genesis 1:26). He is made in the image of God, since his being is in the image of God's being, and his eternal being is in the image of God's eternal being (in the sense that, though not without origin, it is nevertheless without end).[5] He is also made in the likeness of God, since he is good in the likeness of God's goodness, and wise in the likeness of God's wisdom, God being good and wise by nature, and man by grace. Every intelligent nature is created in the image of God, but only the good and the wise attain his likeness.

St. Maximos the Confessor
II, Third Century on Love, sec. 25

He who after the example of God had completed the sixth day with fitting actions and thoughts, and has himself with God's help brought his own actions to a successful conclusion, has in his understanding traversed the condition of all things subject to nature and time and has entered into the mystical contemplation of the eons and the things inherent in them: his sabbath is his intellect's utter and incomprehensible abandonment and transcendence of created beings. But if he is also worthy of the eighth day, he has risen from the dead—that is, from all that is sequent to God, whether sensible or intelligible, expressible or conceivable. He experiences the blessed life of God, who is the only true life, and himself becomes god by deification.

St. Maximos the Confessor
II, First Century on Theology, sec. 54

6 Once again, we are reminded that the whole purpose of the Incarnation is the deification of human beings. This theme is expressed in the Western prayer offered by the priest as he mixes wine and water (representing the divine and human natures of Christ) in the chalice before the mixture is consecrated as the blood of Christ in the Eucharist.

One version of the prayer is this: "O God, who wonderfully created and yet more wonderfully restored the dignity of human nature: Grant that we may share the divine life of him who humbled himself to share our humanity, your Son Jesus Christ our Lord" (*The Book of Common Prayer*).

7 "Love makes man god" refers first to God's love in giving the gift of deification, and second to our love, which is how we cooperate with God's grace in order to become divine. All these techniques are useless without love.

If the divine Logos of God the Father became Son of man, and man so that he might make men gods and the sons of God,[6] let us believe that we shall reach the realm where Christ himself now is; for he is the head of the whole body (Colossians 1:18), and endued with our humanity has gone to the Father as forerunner on our behalf. God will stand "in the midst of the congregation of gods" (Psalm 82:1, LXX)— that is, of those who are saved—distributing the rewards of that realm's blessedness to those found worthy to receive them, not separated from them by any space.

ST. MAXIMOS THE CONFESSOR
II, *SECOND CENTURY ON THEOLOGY*, SEC. 25

The most perfect work of love, and the fulfillment of its activity, is to effect an exchange between those it joins together, which in some measure unites their distinctive characteristics and adapts their respective conditions to each other. Love makes man god, and reveals and manifests God as man, through the single and identical purpose and activity of the will of both. If we are made, as we are, in the image of God (Genesis 1:27), let us become the image of both ourselves and of God; or rather, let us all become the image of the one whole God, bearing nothing earthly in ourselves, so that we may consort with God and become gods, receiving from God our existence as gods. For in this way the divine gifts and the presence of divine peace are honored.[7]

ST. MAXIMOS THE CONFESSOR
II, *FIRST CENTURY OF VARIOUS TEXTS*, SEC. 28

8 Maximos makes it clear that we are not gods by nature, but by
grace. He also refers to "all things" being deified. The Eastern tradition understands salvation as cosmic in scale—all of creation is to be
redeemed, sanctified, transfigured. Everything will participate in and
reveal the glory of God.

9 Maximos asserts here that deification does not mean that we take on
God's nature or that we are simply merged into Divinity. The East
makes a distinction between God's essence and God's energies. The latter are God's actions and gifts, and they are truly God—so when God
gives us grace, we are receiving nothing less than God himself. But
God's essence is and will always be unknowable to anything outside
of God, including the divinized human being. This distinction maintains
the difference between God and creation while nonetheless providing
for a real participation in God.

By intelligence we should be stimulated to overcome our ignorance and to seek the one and only God by means of spiritual knowledge; through desire—through a passion of self-love that has been purified—we should be drawn in longing to the one God; and, with an incensive power divorced from all tyrannical propensity, we should struggle to attain God alone. From these three powers of the soul we should actualize that divine and blessed love on account of which they exist, that love that joins the devout man to God and reveals him to be a god.

St. Maximos the Confessor
II, First Century of Various Texts, sec. 32

God made us so that we might become "partakers of the divine nature" (2 Peter 1:4) and sharers in His eternity, and so that we might come to be like him (1 John 3:2) through deification by grace. It is through deification that all things are reconstituted and achieve their permanence; and it is for its [deification's] sake that what is not is brought into being and given existence.[8]

St. Maximos the Confessor
II, First Century of Various Texts, sec. 42

A sure warrant for looking forward with hope to the deification of human nature is provided by the Incarnation of God, which makes man god to the same degree as God himself became man. For it is clear that he who became man without sin (Hebrews 4:15) will divinize human nature without changing it into the divine nature, and will raise it up for his own sake to the same degree as he lowered himself for man's sake. This is what St. Paul teaches mystically when he says, "that in the ages to come he might display the overflowing richness of his grace" (Ephesians 2:7).[9]

St. Maximos the Confessor
II, First Century of Various Texts, sec. 62

10 Some Christians believe that God only wills the salvation of some human beings, and further, that the saving acts of Christ were intended only for those destined to be saved. But the Orthodox Church has always believed that God's salvific will is universal; that is, it is God's will that all be saved (1 Timothy 2:4).

11 Maximos expresses the Eastern view that the saving acts of Christ, including his death on the cross, are all aimed at our deification. This is strikingly different from the later Western view associated with Anselm of Canterbury (1033–1109), known variously as the "substitutionary" or "penal" model of the Atonement. According to this model, Christ dies on the cross in our place and God chooses to look on us sinners as Christ; we are not changed, but God "imputes" the righteousness of Christ to us. The cross is for the forgiveness of our sins. The older Eastern view sees the Atonement in the wider context of the Incarnation and our deification.

God, who yearns for the salvation of all men and hungers for their deification, withers their conceit like the unfruitful fig tree (Matthew 21:19–21).[10]

ST. MAXIMOS THE CONFESSOR
II, *FIRST CENTURY OF VARIOUS TEXTS*, SEC. 74

For created things are not by nature able to accomplish deification, since they cannot grasp God. To bestow a consonant measure of deification on created beings is within the power of divine grace alone. Grace irradiates nature with a supernatural light and by the transcendence of its glory raises nature above its natural limits.

ST. MAXIMOS THE CONFESSOR
II, *FIRST CENTURY OF VARIOUS TEXTS*, SEC. 76

He who aspires to divine realities willingly allows providence to lead him by principles of wisdom toward the grace of deification. He who does not so aspire is drawn, by the just judgment of God and against his will, away from evil by various forms of discipline. The first, as a lover of God, is deified by providence; the second, although a lover of matter, is held back from perdition by God's judgment. For since God is goodness itself, he heals those who desire it through the principles of wisdom, and through various forms of discipline cures those who are sluggish in virtue.

ST. MAXIMOS THE CONFESSOR
II, *THIRD CENTURY OF VARIOUS TEXTS*, SEC. 36

To reconcile us with the Father, at his Father's wish the Son deliberately gave himself to death on our behalf so that, just as he consented to be dishonored for our sake by assuming our passions, to an equal degree he might glorify us with the beauty of his own divinity.[11]

ST. MAXIMOS THE CONFESSOR
II, *FOURTH CENTURY OF VARIOUS TEXTS*, SEC. 50

12 Part of the wider context of the Incarnation is the fact of the Incarnation. That is to say, one of the problems facing humanity before the Incarnation was the fact of our fallen human nature. God's answer to that is the Incarnation itself, for, from the moment Christ wed his divine nature to human nature in the womb of the Virgin Mary, human nature would never be the same. Without this first step of uniting our nature to God's, the cross and Resurrection would be meaningless and ineffectual for our salvation.

13 Maximos reminds us that salvation and deification are not a one-sided affair. It is true that we cannot earn or achieve our salvation on our own—it is a gift from God. At the same time, however, God does not and will not deify us against our will. The initiative is God's: God offers us deifying grace. But we must accept God's offer and actively cooperate with God's grace.

The law of grace directly teaches those who are led by it to imitate God himself. For—if it is permitted to speak in this way—despite the fact that because of sin we were his enemies, God loved us so much more than himself that, although he is beyond every being, he entered without changing into our being, supra-essentially took on human nature, became man, and, wishing to reveal himself as a man among men, did not refuse to make his own the penalty we pay. And as in his providence he became man, so he deified us by grace, in this way teaching us not only to cleave to one another naturally and to love others spiritually as ourselves, but also, like God, to be more concerned for others than for ourselves, and as proof of our love for each other readily to choose, as virtue enjoins, to die for others. For, as Scripture tells us, there is no greater love than to lay down one's life for a friend (John 15:13).**12**

ST. MAXIMOS THE CONFESSOR
II, *FIFTH CENTURY OF VARIOUS TEXTS*, SEC. 22

Deification through assumption into the Divine is produced by perfect love and an intellect voluntarily blinded, because of its transcendent state, to anything that is sequent to God.

ST. MAXIMOS THE CONFESSOR
II, *FIFTH CENTURY OF VARIOUS TEXTS*, SEC. 93

Created man cannot become a son of God and god by grace through deification, unless he is first through his own free choice begotten in the Spirit by means of the self-loving and independent power dwelling naturally within him. The first man neglected this divinizing, divine, and immaterial birth by choosing what is manifest and delectable to the senses in preference to the spiritual blessings that were as yet unrevealed. In this way he fittingly condemned himself to a bodily generation that is without choice, that is material, and that is subject to death.**13**

ST. MAXIMOS THE CONFESSOR
II, *FIFTH CENTURY OF VARIOUS TEXTS*, SEC. 97

14 While prayer takes many forms and seemingly different aims (such as adoration, confession, thanksgiving, petition, and intercession), Maximos exhorts us to make deification the true aim of our prayer. This, he says, will only increase our love for God.

15 Just as theology properly understood *is* the Trinity, it is the knowledge and worship of the Trinity that *is* our deification.

The Logos bestows adoption on us when he grants us that birth and deification, which, transcending nature, comes by grace from above through the Spirit. The guarding and preservation of this in God depends on the resolve of those thus born: on their sincere acceptance of the grace bestowed on them and, through the practice of the commandments, on their cultivation of the beauty given to them by grace.

St. Maximos the Confessor
II, *On the Lord's Prayer*

When we pray, let our aim be this mystery of deification, which shows us what we were once like, and what the self-emptying of the only-begotten Son through the flesh has now made us; which shows us, that is, the depths to which we were dragged down by the weight of sin, and the heights to which we have been raised by his compassionate hand. In this way we shall come to have greater love for him who has prepared this salvation for us with such wisdom.[14]

St. Maximos the Confessor
II, *On the Lord's Prayer*

The knowledge of the holy and coessential Trinity is the sanctification and deification of men and angels.[15]

St. Thalassios the Libyan
II, *On Love, Self-control, and Life in Accordance
with the Intellect*, First Century, sec. 100

16 While the texts of the *Philokalia* happen to be addressed largely to monks, Peter of Damaskos here makes clear that deification is not limited to monks—it is intended for all God's creatures. Whatever our "time, place, or activity" we are called to grow into the likeness of God. In the words of Basil the Great, the human being is "the creature who has received an order to become god."

This is the beginning of our salvation; by our free choice we abandon our own wishes and thoughts and do what God wishes and thinks. If we succeed in doing this, there is no object, no activity or place in the whole of creation that can prevent us from becoming what God from the beginning has wished us to be: that is to say, according to his image and likeness, gods by adoption through grace, dispassionate, just, good, and wise, whether we are rich or poor, married or unmarried, in authority and free or under obedience and in bondage—in short, whatever our time, place, or activity. That is why, alike before the Law, under the Law and under grace, there have been many righteous men—men who preferred the knowledge of God and his will to their own thoughts and wishes.[16]

ST. PETER OF DAMASKOS
III, *A TREASURY OF KNOWLEDGE*, INTRODUCTION

Through the wisdom and indwelling of the Holy Spirit and through adoption to sonship, we are crucified with Christ and buried with him, and we rise with him and ascend with him spiritually by imitating his way of life in this world. To speak simply, we become gods by adoption through grace, receiving the pledge of eternal blessedness, as St. Gregory the Theologian says.

ST. PETER OF DAMASKOS
III, *A TREASURY OF KNOWLEDGE*, INTRODUCTION

17 Symeon identifies deification as the underlying message of the Holy Scriptures, a message we often fail to recognize. If this was true in Symeon's day, it is all the more true in ours. Only with the patristic and Eastern monastic revivals of the twentieth century have we begun to recover this way of understanding the Bible.

18 In Orthodox anthropology, our sinful condition is not our true nature. We are made in the image of God, which is our true nature. We can follow our true nature with the help of God. We are not, as some have taught, "totally depraved" by nature.

What is the purpose of the Incarnation of the Divine Logos, which is proclaimed throughout the Scriptures, about which we read and that yet we do not recognize? Surely it is that he has shared in what is ours so as to make us participants of what he is. For the Son of God became the Son of man in order to make us human beings sons of God, raising us up by grace to what he is by nature, giving us a new birth in the Holy Spirit and leading us directly into the kingdom of heaven. Or, rather, he gives us the grace to possess this kingdom within ourselves (Luke 17:21), so that not merely do we hope to enter it, but being in full possession of it, we can affirm: "Our life is hid with Christ in God" (Colossians 3:3).[17]

ST. SYMEON THE NEW THEOLOGIAN
IV, *ONE HUNDRED AND FIFTY-THREE PRACTICAL*
AND THEOLOGICAL TEXTS, SEC. 108

If when aroused and active a man's incensive, appetitive, and intelligent powers spontaneously operate in accordance with nature, they make him wholly godlike and divine, sound in his actions and never in any way dislodged from nature's bedrock. But if, betraying his own nature, he follows a course that is contrary to nature, these same powers will turn him, as we have said, into a polymorphic monster, compounded of many self-antagonistic parts.[18]

NIKITAS STITHATOS
IV, *ON THE PRACTICE OF THE VIRTUES: ONE HUNDRED TEXTS*, SEC. 15

19 The Eucharist is an indispensable element of our deification. Through it, Nikitas says, God "refashions us in himself, wholly deifying us." We see this in the early Western tradition as well. Augustine of Hippo has Christ say: "I am the food of grown men and women. Grow, and you shall feed upon me. You will not change me into yourself, as you change food into your flesh, but you will be changed into me" (*Confessions*, Book VII:10).

The Logos of God, having taken flesh and given our nature subsistence in himself, becoming perfect man, entirely free from sin, has as perfect God refashioned our nature and made it divine. As Logos of the primal Intellect and God, he has united himself to our intelligence, giving it wings so that we may conceive divine, exalted thoughts. Because he is fire, he has with true divine fire steeled the incensive power of the soul against hostile passions and demons. Aspiration of all intelligent beings and slaker of all desire, he has in his deep-seated love dilated the appetitive aspect of the soul so that it can partake of the blessings of eternal life. Having thus renewed the whole man in himself, he restores it in an act of re-creation that leaves no grounds for any reproach against the Creator-Logos.

NIKITAS STITHATOS
IV, *ON THE INNER NATURE OF THINGS AND*
ON THE PURIFICATION OF THE INTELLECT, SEC. 93

If, then, tested in the labor of virtue and purified by tears, we come forward and eat of this bread and drink of this cup, the divine-human Logos in his gentleness is commixed with our two natural faculties, with our soul and body; and as God incarnate—one with us in essence with regard to our human nature—he totally refashions us in himself, wholly deifying us through divine knowledge and uniting us with himself as his brothers, conformed to him who is God coessential with the Father.[19]

NIKITAS STITHATOS
IV, *ON THE INNER NATURE OF THINGS AND*
ON THE PURIFICATION OF THE INTELLECT, SEC. 95

+ "Union with God is not a subsidiary issue in faith or doctrine. It is the basis of all faith and doctrine. It is the ultimate aim of God for sending his only Son to the world to become man: 'For he has made known to us in all wisdom and insight the mystery of his will, according to his purpose which he set forth in Christ as a plan for the fullness of time, to unite all things in Christ, things in heaven and on earth' (Ephesians 1:9–10). So the mystery of union between mankind and Christ is the ultimate aim of the incarnation, the crucifixion, the resurrection—nay, of creation in full."

—Matthew the Poor, *Orthodox Prayer Life: The Inner Way*

20 We are not saved or deified alone, but in the community that is the Church, the body of Christ. In order to be deified, we must be "joined together in the union of love."

When through the practice of the virtues we attain a spiritual knowledge of created things we have achieved the first stage on the path to deification. We achieve the second stage when—initiated through the contemplation of the spiritual essences of created things—we perceive the hidden mysteries of God. We achieve the third stage when we are united and interfused with the primordial light. It is then that we reach the goal of all ascetic and contemplative activity.

NIKITAS STITHATOS
IV, *ON SPIRITUAL KNOWLEDGE, LOVE, AND*
THE PERFECTION OF LIVING, SEC. 31

Those who, as a result of their purity and their knowledge of things divine, participate in this dignity are assimilated to God, "conformed to the image of His Son" (Romans 8:29), through their exalted and spiritual concentration upon the divine. Thus, they become gods to other men on earth. These others in their turn, perfected in virtue by purification through their divine intelligence and through sacred intercourse with God, participate according to their proficiency and the degree of their purification in the same deification as their brethren, and they commune with them in the God of unity. In this way all of them, joined together in the union of love, are unceasingly united with the one God; and God, the source of all holy works and totally free from any indictment because of his work of creation, abides in the midst of gods (Psalm 82:1, LXX), God by nature among gods by adoption.[20]

NIKITAS STITHATOS
IV, *ON SPIRITUAL KNOWLEDGE, LOVE, AND*
THE PERFECTION OF LIVING, SEC. 33

21 Theoliptos says that the practice of the virtues and the invocation of the Lord are how we prepare ourselves to cooperate with God's deifying grace. Moreover, knowing and loving are seen as inseparable.

+ "Sharing wholly in our poverty, you have made divine our earthly nature through your union with it and participation in it."

—Orthodox hymn for the Nativity of Christ

And as Adam, molded by God's hand from dust, became through
divine spiration a living soul, so the intellect molded by the virtues
and repeatedly invoking the Lord with a pure mind and an ardent
spirit, is divinely transformed, quickened, and deified through
knowing and loving God.[21]

THEOLIPTOS, METROPOLITAN OF PHILADELPHIA
IV, *TEXTS*, SEC. 2

For according to St. Basil, "Spirit-bearing souls, when illumined by the
Spirit, both become spiritual themselves and shed forth grace upon
others. From this comes foreknowledge of things future, understanding
of mysteries, apprehension of things hidden, distribution of spiritual
gifts, citizenship in heaven, the dance with the angels, unending joy,
divine largesse, likeness to God, and the desire of all desires, to
become god."

ST. GREGORY PALAMAS
IV, *TOPICS OF NATURAL AND THEOLOGICAL SCIENCE
AND ON THE MORAL AND ASCETIC LIFE*, SEC. 76

In the incomparable and superabundance of his goodness, he who
brought forth and adorned the universe established it as multiform. He
willed that some things should simply possess being, while others
should possess life in addition to being. Of these latter he willed that
some should possess noetic life, that others should enjoy merely a
sensible life, while others again should possess a life mingled with
both. When this last category of beings had received from him
rational and noetic life, he willed that by the free inclination of their
will toward him they should achieve union with him and thus live in a
divine and supranatural manner, having been vouchsafed his deifying
grace and energy.

ST. GREGORY PALAMAS
IV, *TOPICS OF NATURAL AND THEOLOGICAL SCIENCE
AND ON THE MORAL AND ASCETIC LIFE*, SEC. 91

22 Gregory emphasizes that all that we can do by our efforts is to make ourselves "fit" for union with God. We cannot achieve salvation by our own efforts. Deification is a gift from God, a gift of God himself to us. We can only prepare to receive it and do what is necessary to accept it.

23 Gregory is the Orthodox theologian who first elaborated at length the distinction between God's nature and God's energies. While protecting the distinction between God and the creature, Gregory maintains that participation in God's energies is a real participation in God, saying that "the saints in their entirety penetrate God entirely."

This resplendence and deifying energy of God, which deifies those
who participate in it, constitutes divine grace, but it is not the nature
of God. This does not mean that God's nature is distant from those
who have received grace … for God's nature is everywhere; but it
means that it is not participable, since no created thing … is capable
of participating in it. The divine energy and grace of the Spirit, being
everywhere present and remaining inseparable from the Spirit, is
imparticipable, as though absent, for those who, on account of their
impurity, are unfit to participate in it. Just as faces, so it is said, are not
reflected by every material, but only by such materials as possess
smoothness and transparency, so the energy of the Spirit is not found
in all souls, but only in those possessing no perversity or
deviousness.[22]

ST. GREGORY PALAMAS
IV, *TOPICS OF NATURAL AND THEOLOGICAL SCIENCE AND
ON THE MORAL AND ASCETIC LIFE*, SEC. 93

The grace of deification is … above nature, virtue, and knowledge
and, according to St. Maximos, all such things infinitely fall short of it.
For all the virtue we can attain and such imitation of God as lies in our
power does no more than fit us for union with the Deity, but it is
through grace that this ineffable union is actually accomplished.
Through grace, God in his entirety penetrates the saints in their
entirety, and the saints in their entirety penetrate God entirely,
exchanging the whole of him for themselves, and acquiring him alone
as the reward of their ascent toward him; for he embraces them as the
soul embraces the body, enabling them to be in him as his own
members.[23]

ST. GREGORY PALAMAS
IV, *THE DECLARATION OF THE HOLY MOUNTAIN IN DEFENSE OF THOSE
WHO DEVOUTLY PRACTICE A LIFE OF STILLNESS*, SEC. 2

Notes

1. Gleb Pokrovsky, trans., *The Way of a Pilgrim: Annotated and Explained* (Woodstock, Vt.: SkyLight Paths, 2001), 15, 17.
2. John Chryssavgis, *Light through Darkness: The Orthodox Tradition* (Maryknoll, N.Y.: Orbis Books, 2004), 87–88.
3. Vladimir Lossky, *The Mystical Theology of the Eastern Church* (Crestwood, N.Y.: St. Vladimir's Seminary Press, 1976), 8–9.
4. Philip Sherrard, *Christianity: Lineaments of a Sacred Tradition* (Brookline, Mass.: Holy Cross Orthodox Press, 1998), 264.

Suggestions for Further Reading

English Editions of the *Philokalia*

The Philokalia: The Complete Text. Translated and edited by G. E. H. Palmer, Philip Sherrard, and Kallistos Ware. 5 vols. London: Faber and Faber, 1979–2007. This is the only complete English translation of *The Philokalia of the Neptic Fathers,* produced by St. Nikodimos of the Holy Mountain and St. Makarios of Corinth. The first four volumes appeared in 1979, 1981, 1984, and 1995. The fifth and final volume is expected in 2007.

Writings from the Philokalia on Prayer of the Heart. Translated by E. Kadloubovsky and E. M. Palmer. London: Faber and Faber, 1992. This is a one-volume selection and reordering of texts from the *Philokalia* edited and translated into Slavonic by St. Paissy Velichovsky (1722–1794) and later translated into Russian by St. Theophan the Recluse (1815–1894). It is known in Russian as *Dobrotolubiye,* which, like the Greek word *Philokalia,* means "the love of the beautiful." This edition reflects the order of the *Philokalia* texts recommended in the anonymous classic of Russian spirituality, *The Way of a Pilgrim.*

Other Works

Chariton of Valamo, Igumen. *The Art of Prayer: An Orthodox Anthology.* Translated by E. Kadloubovsky and E. M. Palmer, and edited with an introduction by Timothy Ware. London: Faber and Faber, 1997. This is a useful anthology of texts on prayer from the Greek and Russian Orthodox traditions.

Colliander, Tito. *The Way of the Ascetics.* Crestwood, N.Y.: St. Vladimir's Seminary Press, 1985. A remarkable yet brief introduction to Orthodox spirituality.

Golitzin, Alexander, ed. *The Living Witness of the Holy Mountain: Contemporary Voices from Mount Athos.* South Canaan, Pa.: St. Tikhon's Seminary Press, 1995. A useful collection compiled by an Athonite monk.

Lossky, Vladimir. *The Mystical Theology of the Eastern Church.* Crestwood, N.Y.: St. Vladimir's Seminary Press, 1976. A twentieth-century classic in which Lossky shows the fundamental unity of dogmatic and mystical theology.

Markides, Kyriacos C. *The Mountain of Silence: A Search for Orthodox Spirituality.* New York: Doubleday, 2001. A very readable introduction to the spiritual traditions of Mount Athos, based on the author's conversations with Father Maximos, an Athonite monk.

Matthew the Poor (Mata El-Meskeen). *Orthodox Prayer Life: The Interior Way.* Crestwood, N.Y.: St. Vladimir's Seminary Press, 2004. A superior introduction consisting of a collection of patristic texts on prayer with commentary by a leading monk of the Coptic Orthodox Church in Egypt.

Pennington, M. Basil. *The Monks of Mount Athos: A Western Monk's Extraordinary Spiritual Journey on Eastern Holy Ground.* Woodstock, Vt.: SkyLight Paths Publishing, 2003. A spiritual exploration of the Holy Mountain made by a Trappist monk of the Roman Catholic Church.

Staniloae, Dumitru. *Orthodox Spirituality: A Practical Guide for the Faithful and a Definitive Manual for the Scholar.* South Canaan, Pa.: St. Tikhon's Seminary Press, 2002. This is a thorough introduction to Orthodox spirituality by a gifted twentieth-century theologian who also translated the *Philokalia* into Romanian.

Ware, Kallistos. *The Orthodox Way,* rev. ed. Crestwood, N.Y.: St. Vladimir's Seminary Press, 1995. A spiritual introduction to Orthodoxy to complement the author's earlier work, *The Orthodox Church,* which focused on Orthodox history and theology.

Ware, Timothy [later Kallistos]. *The Orthodox Church.* New York: Penguin, 1993. Probably the best and most popular introduction to Eastern Orthodoxy in the English language.

The Way of a Pilgrim: Annotated and Explained. Translated and annotated by Gleb Pokrovsky. Woodstock, Vt.: SkyLight Paths Publishing, 2001. This Russian classic follows a pilgrim's introduction to the practice of the Jesus Prayer and his immersion into hesychasm.

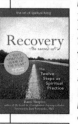

Spiritual Practice

Laugh Your Way to Grace: Reclaiming the Spiritual Power of Humor
by Rev. Susan Sparks A powerful, humorous case for laughter as a spiritual, healing path. 6 x 9, 176 pp, Quality PB, 978-1-59473-280-5 **$16.99**

Haiku—The Sacred Art: A Spiritual Practice in Three Lines
by Margaret D. McGee Introduces haiku as a simple and effective way of tapping into the sacred moments that permeate everyday living.
5½ x 8½, 192 pp, Quality PB, 978-1-59473-269-0 **$16.99**

Dance—The Sacred Art: The Joy of Movement as a Spiritual Practice
by Cynthia Winton-Henry Invites all of us, regardless of experience, into the possibility of dance/movement as a spiritual practice.
5½ x 8½, 224 pp, Quality PB, 978-1-59473-268-3 **$16.99**

Spiritual Adventures in the Snow: Skiing & Snowboarding as Renewal for Your Soul *by Dr. Marcia McFee and Rev. Karen Foster; Foreword by Paul Arthur*
Explores snow sports as tangible experiences of the spiritual essence of our bodies and the earth. 5½ x 8½, 208 pp, Quality PB, 978-1-59473-270-6 **$16.99**

Recovery—The Sacred Art: The Twelve Steps as Spiritual Practice
by Rami Shapiro; Foreword by Joan Borysenko, PhD Uniquely interprets the Twelve Steps of Alcoholics Anonymous to speak to everyone seeking a freer and more God-centered life. 5½ x 8½, 240 pp, Quality PB, 978-1-59473-259-1 **$16.99**

Hospitality—The Sacred Art: Discovering the Hidden Spiritual Power of Invitation and Welcome *by Rev. Nanette Sawyer; Foreword by Rev. Dirk Ficca*
5½ x 8½, 208 pp, Quality PB, 978-1-59473-228-7 **$16.99**

Labyrinths from the Outside In: Walking to Spiritual Insight—A Beginner's Guide
by Donna Schaper and Carole Ann Camp
6 x 9, 208 pp, b/w illus. and photos, Quality PB, 978-1-893361-18-8 **$16.95**

Practicing the Sacred Art of Listening: A Guide to Enrich Your Relationships and Kindle Your Spiritual Life *by Kay Lindahl* 8 x 8, 176 pp, Quality PB, 978-1-893361-85-0 **$16.95**

Running—The Sacred Art: Preparing to Practice *by Dr. Warren A. Kay; Foreword by Kristin Armstrong* 5½ x 8½, 160 pp, Quality PB, 978-1-59473-227-0 **$16.99**

The Sacred Art of Bowing: Preparing to Practice
by Andi Young 5½ x 8½, 128 pp, b/w illus., Quality PB, 978-1-893361-82-9 **$14.95**

The Sacred Art of Chant: Preparing to Practice
by Ana Hernández 5½ x 8½, 192 pp, Quality PB, 978-1-59473-036-8 **$15.99**

The Sacred Art of Fasting: Preparing to Practice
by Thomas Ryan, CSP 5½ x 8½, 192 pp, Quality PB, 978-1-59473-078-8 **$15.99**

The Sacred Art of Forgiveness: Forgiving Ourselves and Others through God's Grace
by Marcia Ford 8 x 8, 176 pp, Quality PB, 978-1-59473-175-4 **$16.99**

The Sacred Art of Listening: Forty Reflections for Cultivating a Spiritual Practice
by Kay Lindahl; Illustrations by Amy Schnapper 8 x 8, 160 pp, b/w illus., Quality PB, 978-1-893361-44-7 **$16.99**

The Sacred Art of Lovingkindness: Preparing to Practice
by Rabbi Rami Shapiro; Foreword by Marcia Ford 5½ x 8½, 176 pp, Quality PB, 978-1-59473-151-8 **$16.99**

Thanking & Blessing—The Sacred Art: Spiritual Vitality through Gratefulness
by Jay Marshall, PhD; Foreword by Philip Gulley 5½ x 8½, 176 pp, Quality PB, 978-1-59473-231-7 **$16.99**

Sacred Texts—SkyLight Illuminations Series

Offers today's spiritual seeker an enjoyable entry into the great classic texts of the world's spiritual traditions. Each classic is presented in an accessible translation, with facing pages of guided commentary from experts, giving you the keys you need to understand the history, context and meaning of the text.

CHRISTIANITY

The End of Days: Essential Selections from Apocalyptic Texts—
Annotated & Explained *Annotation by Robert G. Clouse*
Helps you understand the complex Christian visions of the end of the world.
5½ x 8½, 224 pp, Quality PB, 978-1-59473-170-9 **$16.99**

The Hidden Gospel of Matthew: Annotated & Explained
Translation & Annotation by Ron Miller Takes you deep into the text cherished around the world to discover the words and events that have the strongest connection to the historical Jesus. 5½ x 8½, 272 pp, Quality PB, 978-1-59473-038-2 **$16.99**

The Infancy Gospels of Jesus: Apocryphal Tales from the Childhoods of Mary and Jesus—Annotated & Explained
Translation & Annotation by Stevan Davies; Foreword by A. Edward Siecienski, PhD
A startling presentation of the early lives of Mary, Jesus and other biblical figures that will amuse and surprise you. 5½ x 8½, 176 pp, Quality PB, 978-1-59473-258-4 **$16.99**

The Lost Sayings of Jesus: Teachings from Ancient Christian, Jewish, Gnostic and Islamic Sources—Annotated & Explained
Translation & Annotation by Andrew Phillip Smith; Foreword by Stephan A. Hoeller
This collection of more than three hundred sayings depicts Jesus as a Wisdom teacher who speaks to people of all faiths as a mystic and spiritual master.
5½ x 8½, 240 pp, Quality PB, 978-1-59473-172-3 **$16.99**

Philokalia: The Eastern Christian Spiritual Texts—Selections Annotated & Explained *Annotation by Allyne Smith; Translation by G. E. H. Palmer, Phillip Sherrard and Bishop Kallistos Ware*
The first approachable introduction to the wisdom of the Philokalia, the classic text of Eastern Christian spirituality. 5½ x 8½, 240 pp, Quality PB, 978-1-59473-103-7 **$16.99**

The Sacred Writings of Paul: Selections Annotated & Explained
Translation & Annotation by Ron Miller Leads you into the exciting immediacy of Paul's teachings. 5½ x 8½, 224 pp, Quality PB, 978-1-59473-213-3 **$16.99**

Saint Augustine of Hippo: Selections from *Confessions* and Other Essential Writings—Annotated & Explained
Annotation by Joseph T. Kelley, PhD; Translation by the Augustinian Heritage Institute
Provides insight into the mind and heart of this foundational Christian figure.
5½ x 8½, 272 pp, Quality PB, 978-1-59473-282-9 **$16.99**

Sex Texts from the Bible: Selections Annotated & Explained
Translation & Annotation by Teresa J. Hornsby; Foreword by Amy-Jill Levine
Demystifies the Bible's ideas on gender roles, marriage, sexual orientation, virginity, lust and sexual pleasure. 5½ x 8½, 208 pp, Quality PB, 978-1-59473-217-1 **$16.99**

Spiritual Writings on Mary: Annotated & Explained
Annotation by Mary Ford-Grabowsky; Foreword by Andrew Harvey
Examines the role of Mary, the mother of Jesus, as a source of inspiration in history and in life today. 5½ x 8½, 288 pp, Quality PB, 978-1-59473-001-6 **$16.99**

The Way of a Pilgrim: The Jesus Prayer Journey—Annotated & Explained
Translation & Annotation by Gleb Pokrovsky; Foreword by Andrew Harvey
This classic of Russian Orthodox spirituality is the delightful account of one man who sets out to learn the prayer of the heart, also known as the "Jesus prayer."
5½ x 8½, 160 pp, Illus., Quality PB, 978-1-893361-31-7 **$14.95**

Sacred Texts—continued

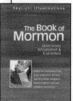

MORMONISM

The Book of Mormon: Selections Annotated & Explained

Annotation by Jana Riess; Foreword by Phyllis Tickle Explores the sacred epic that is cherished by more than twelve million members of the LDS church as the keystone of their faith. 5½ x 8½ , 272 pp, Quality PB, 978-1-59473-076-4 **$16.99**

NATIVE AMERICAN

Native American Stories of the Sacred: Annotated & Explained

Retold & Annotated by Evan T. Pritchard Intended for more than entertainment, these teaching tales contain elegantly simple illustrations of time-honored truths. 5½ x 8½, 272 pp, Quality PB, 978-1-59473-112-9 **$16.99**

GNOSTICISM

Gnostic Writings on the Soul: Annotated & Explained

Translation & Annotation by Andrew Phillip Smith; Foreword by Stephan A. Hoeller Reveals the inspiring ways your soul can remember and return to its unique, divine purpose. 5½ x 8½, 144 pp, Quality PB, 978-1-59473-220-1 **$16.99**

The Gospel of Philip: Annotated & Explained

Translation & Annotation by Andrew Phillip Smith; Foreword by Stevan Davies Reveals otherwise unrecorded sayings of Jesus and fragments of Gnostic mythology. 5½ x 8½, 160 pp, Quality PB, 978-1-59473-111-2 **$16.99**

The Gospel of Thomas: Annotated & Explained

Translation & Annotation by Stevan Davies; Foreword by Andrew Harvey Sheds new light on the origins of Christianity and portrays Jesus as a wisdom-loving sage. 5½ x 8½, 192 pp, Quality PB, 978-1-893361-45-4 **$16.99**

The Secret Book of John: The Gnostic Gospel—Annotated & Explained

Translation & Annotation by Stevan Davies The most significant and influential text of the ancient Gnostic religion. 5½ x 8½, 208 pp, Quality PB, 978-1-59473-082-5 **$16.99**

JUDAISM

The Divine Feminine in Biblical Wisdom Literature

Selections Annotated & Explained

Translation & Annotation by Rabbi Rami Shapiro; Foreword by Rev. Cynthia Bourgeault, PhD Uses the Hebrew Bible and Wisdom literature to explain Sophia's way of wisdom and illustrate Her creative energy. 5½ x 8½, 240 pp, Quality PB, 978-1-59473-109-9 **$16.99**

Ethics of the Sages: Pirke Avot—Annotated & Explained

Translation & Annotation by Rabbi Rami Shapiro Clarifies the ethical teachings of the early Rabbis. 5½ x 8½, 192 pp, Quality PB, 978-1-59473-207-2 **$16.99**

Hasidic Tales: Annotated & Explained

Translation & Annotation by Rabbi Rami Shapiro Introduces the legendary tales of the impassioned Hasidic rabbis, presenting them as stories rather than as parables. 5½ x 8½, 240 pp, Quality PB, 978-1-893361-86-5 **$16.95**

The Hebrew Prophets: Selections Annotated & Explained

Translation & Annotation by Rabbi Rami Shapiro; Foreword by Rabbi Zalman M. Schachter-Shalomi Makes the wisdom of these timeless teachers accessible. 5½ x 8½, 224 pp, Quality PB, 978-1-59473-037-5 **$16.99**

Tanya, the Masterpiece of Hasidic Wisdom: Selections Annotated & Explained *Translation & Annotation by Rabbi Rami Shapiro; Foreword by Rabbi Zalman M. Schachter-Shalomi* Clarifies one of the most powerful and potentially transformative books of Jewish wisdom. 5½ x 8½, 240 pp, Quality PB, 978-1-59473-275-1 **$16.99**

Zohar: Annotated & Explained

Translation & Annotation by Daniel C. Matt; Foreword by Andrew Harvey Brings together the most important teachings of the Zohar, the canonical text of Jewish mystical tradition. 5½ x 8½, 176 pp, Quality PB, 978-1-893361-51-5 **$15.99**

Sacred Texts—continued

ISLAM

Ghazali on the Principles of Islamic Spirituality
Selections from *Forty Foundations of Religion*—Annotated & Explained
Translation & Annotation by Aaron Spevack, PhD
Makes the core message of this influential spiritual master relevant to anyone seeking a balanced understanding of Islam.
5½ x 8¼, 208 pp (est), Quality PB, 978-1-59473-284-3 **$16.99**

The Qur'an and Sayings of Prophet Muhammad
Selections Annotated & Explained
Annotation by Sohaib N. Sultan; Translation by Yusuf Ali, Revised by Sohaib N. Sultan
Foreword by Jane I. Smith
Presents the foundational wisdom of Islam in an easy-to-use format.
5½ x 8¼, 256 pp, Quality PB, 978-1-59473-222-5 **$16.99**

Rumi and Islam: Selections from His Stories, Poems, and Discourses—
Annotated & Explained
Translation & Annotation by Ibrahim Gamard
Focuses on Rumi's place within the Sufi tradition of Islam, providing insight into the mystical side of the religion.
5½ x 8¼, 240 pp, Quality PB, 978-1-59473-002-3 **$15.99**

EASTERN RELIGIONS

The Art of War—Spirituality for Conflict
Annotated & Explained
by Sun Tzu; Annotation by Thomas Huynh; Translation by Thomas Huynh and the Editors at Sonshi.com; Foreword by Marc Benioff; Preface by Thomas Cleary
Highlights principles that encourage a perceptive and spiritual approach to conflict.
5½ x 8¼, 256 pp, Quality PB, 978-1-59473-244-7 **$16.99**

Bhagavad Gita: Annotated & Explained
Translation by Shri Purohit Swami; Annotation by Kendra Crossen Burroughs
Presents the classic text's teachings—with no previous knowledge of Hinduism required. 5½ x 8¼, 192 pp, Quality PB, 978-1-893361-28-7 **$16.95**

Dhammapada: Annotated & Explained
Translation by Max Müller, revised by Jack Maguire; Annotation by Jack Maguire
Contains all of Buddhism's key teachings, plus commentary that explains all the names, terms and references. 5½ x 8¼, 160 pp, b/w photos, Quality PB, 978-1-893361-42-3 **$14.95**

Selections from the Gospel of Sri Ramakrishna
Annotated & Explained
Translation by Swami Nikhilananda; Annotation by Kendra Crossen Burroughs
Introduces the fascinating world of the Indian mystic and the universal appeal of his message. 5½ x 8¼, 240 pp, b/w photos, Quality PB, 978-1-893361-46-1 **$16.95**

Tao Te Ching: Annotated & Explained
Translation & Annotation by Derek Lin; Foreword by Lama Surya Das
Introduces an Eastern classic in an accessible, poetic and completely original way.
5½ x 8¼, 208 pp, Quality PB, 978-1-59473-204-1 **$16.99**

STOICISM

The Meditations of Marcus Aurelius
Selections Annotated & Explained
Annotation by Russell McNeil, PhD; Translation by George Long, revised by Russell McNeil, PhD
Ancient Stoic wisdom that speaks vibrantly today about life, business, government and spirit. 5½ x 8¼, 288 pp, Quality PB, 978-1-59473-236-2 **$16.99**

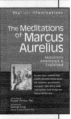

About SKYLIGHT PATHS Publishing

SkyLight Paths Publishing is creating a place where people of different spiritual traditions come together for challenge and inspiration, a place where we can help each other understand the mystery that lies at the heart of our existence.

Through spirituality, our religious beliefs are increasingly becoming a part of our lives—rather than *apart* from our lives. While many of us may be more interested than ever in spiritual growth, we may be less firmly planted in traditional religion. Yet, we do want to deepen our relationship to the sacred, to learn from our own as well as from other faith traditions, and to practice in new ways.

SkyLight Paths sees both believers and seekers as a community that increasingly transcends traditional boundaries of religion and denomination—people wanting to learn from each other, *walking together, finding the way.*

For your information and convenience, at the back of this book we have provided a list of other SkyLight Paths books you might find interesting and useful. They cover the following subjects:

Buddhism / Zen	Global Spiritual	Monasticism
Catholicism	Perspectives	Mysticism
Children's Books	Gnosticism	Poetry
Christianity	Hinduism /	Prayer
Comparative	Vedanta	Religious Etiquette
Religion	Inspiration	Retirement
Current Events	Islam / Sufism	Spiritual Biography
Earth-Based	Judaism	Spiritual Direction
Spirituality	Kabbalah	Spirituality
Enneagram	Meditation	Women's Interest
	Midrash Fiction	Worship